BEHIND DISTILLATION

A research born after the discovery in Cyprus of 2000 BC alembics.

Maria Rosaria Belgiorno

Gianfranco Todisco: Foreword
Ann Harman: Introduction
Amber Roy: Proofreading
Antonio De Strobel:
Computer processing of all illustrations
© Photographs and elaborations:
Fig.: 2, 8, 16, 19, 20, 36, 37, 38, 41, 57, 58,
73, 80, 81, 84, 90, 94, 101, 102, 103, 104,
108, 110, 111, 112, 113, 115, 116, 117,
121, 125, pages. 129, 173, 181
and hard cover.
Simone Iacomini Fig. 105, 106, 107, 109

Sponsored by:
Associazione Culturale "Armonia"
Via Canino 10, Roma, Italy

No part of this book can be reproduced
without previous consent from the publisher

Copyright © 2017 Maria Rosaria Belgiorno
All rights reserved.

ISBN: 978 -9963-2448-1-2
Edited by: Antonio De Strobel
October 2017
Nicosia - Cyprus

DEDICATION

I dedicate this book to my grandchildren Lucilla and Michelangelo, whose birth has rejuvenated my passion for exploring the different aspects of our past.

CONTENTS

	Acknowledgments	7
	Foreword: *Gianfranco Todisco*	9 - 11
	Introduction: *Ann Harman*	13 - 19
I	Technology	21
II	Ancient texts	31
III	Prehistory	45
IV	Simple Apparatuses	51
V	The Strainer	61
VI	Storing pots: a case of comparison between Cyprus and Egypt	65
VII	The alembic head	71
VIII	China	83
IX	Mesopotamia: the cradle of civilizations	91
X	From Anatolia to Slovakia, Sardinia, and Cyprus	113
XI	Aegean	125
XII	Egypt	139
XIII	Pyrgos/Mavroraki Cyprus	151
XIV	A final reflection	175
	References	183

ACKNOWLEDGMENTS

I am indebted to my husband Antonio de Strobel for the edition of this book and to Amber Sophia Roy for the proof reading the manuscript. I also wish to thank Filippo Carinci for giving me the permission to use the drawings of his paper and Angela Antona for allowing me to publish the photographs of the device from Nuraghe La Prisgiona of Arzachena. My special thanks to Vassos Karageorghis who kindly provided me to take the photos and study the tripod from Teratsoudhia, Paphos.

Finally, I am deeply grateful to my friends Gianfranco Todisco and Ann Harman for the foreword and introduction of this book.

FOREWORD

Like every other piece in the history of science, this contribution of Maria Rosaria Belgiorno gives answers, provides additional information and raises new questions; with some very special issues and perhaps unique. The distillation, such as sublimation, is the phenomenon of change of state of matter: liquid-gas-liquid-gas solid -solid-gas for distillation/ sublimation. Today we know the physical events that produce these changes, but this point of arrival has prompted many thousands of years.

During this journey, in the Middle Bronze age, somebody constructs an apparatus for distillation, whose discovery, we are indebted to the author, with a shape that basically will not change until the present day. Anyone looking to the graphic representation of the alembic of Pyrgos (1850 BC) and comparing it with any modern still will realize not only the likeness, but the possible identity of the two devices.

I think there are no other examples in the history of technology that have the same characteristics.

One of the first issues in reconstructions of historical processes is their documentation. Only the first appearance of an attempt of minimally structured knowledge evidence allows intellectual processing and representation theory that workers of all ages build about their activities.

For distillation we must wait, according to the most authoritative and optimistic estimates, the first centuries BC, for written records of this magnitude to come to us. And what we get are Arab copies (probably of 11th century) of in their remote entirely lost Greek manuscripts which embedded of some later tracks. What emerges from the earliest texts tells again the singularity in the world of distillation.

The person who arranged the device for distillation or sublimation is, or we would say today was, a craftsman. However, this figure in classical times was held in low esteem.

Aristotle, for example, if not despised, certainly did not love him. Yet, the artisan who produces and teaches how to build the still we will claim him alchemist, the following of a practice to whom we attribute an immense divine and precious art.

The fact that this philosophical and mystical crucible enters abruptly in manual testing and in the ensuing operations is one more element, which is unprecedented and it is an absolute novelty.

This close link between practice, preparation and theoretical representation of the Action will be something you will perpetuate for many, many centuries; until the present day.

M.R. Belgiorno also takes care of the devices that represent the first traces of literature from the West, but her work goes back further analysing the oldest artefacts to which you can attribute a distilling function. Since the beginning of this journey items and artefacts appear, from several locations and regions, even very far from each other.

Archaeologists are accustomed to this: techniques and artefacts that appear suddenly; fast progress, then silence and then again, maybe far away, someone who picks up the subject where somebody left, taking a step sometimes back, sometimes forward.

For anyone who is not an archaeologist, this non-linearity is puzzling or at least confuses the image of an unstoppable linear progress. Here is another benefit of this work. Some maps provide a graphically fast impact with the places where distillation and sublimation were practiced. The sites considered span East and West, from India and China to the westernmost prehistoric artefacts discovered in Sardinia.

Distant places involve distant cultures, but although sometimes we tie the idea of prehistory to a sort of primitivism less accentuated. People have always moved, have always travelled. A lot. And exchanged ideas and technologies.

The basic problems remain open.

Ex Oriente Lux? What environment produced the artefacts? With what criteria, it is possible to analyse the apparatus for distillation? There were characteristics of material components requiring design and manufacture specific? And above all, the most important question: why the man started to distil, what he cooked, for what kind of production?

Maria Rosaria Belgiorno also debates on these issues, and tells of the apparatus for distillation having discovered. Her perspective is that of a skilled person.

Maybe not every question and definitely not all the answers will come from Archaeology, but without Archaeology questions and answers would be much less.

Gianfranco Todisco

Independent senior researcher; "aromaterapia consapevole": http://pagelous.com/en/pages/52f726eba8fe206f6c03cdb7 http://www.florisco.it; info@florisco.it.

INTRODUCTION

I was captivated by the distillate waters, those that we call hydrosols or hydrolats, over twenty years ago. I was attending an herbal conference in Oregon, USA. The well-known herbalist James Green was demonstrating how to make a rose hydrosol with just a porcelain pot and bowl. In reflection, he was actually using a very ancient technique; little did I know that day would change the direction of my studies and forever put me on the path of distillation and hydrosols. For me the distillate waters were a link between the herbal traditions that I was familiar with and the newly discovered aromatherapy essential oils. Distillation of these waters soon became my passion and as the years have passed I have delved deep into their history.

What exactly is a hydrosol? Hydrosol is a modern term, coined by the American aromatherapist Jeanne Rose to describe the aqueous portion of a distillation of plants. In her words, "'Hydro' means water and 'sol' means solution. Thus, the word **hydrosol** means the watery solution of the distillation that contains both the water-soluble plant components and micro-drops of essential oil -- the hydrosol." Throughout the centuries these distillate waters have had many names, some of the oldest references called them the Waters of ____, simply filling the blank with whatever herb was being distilled, such as the Water of Elder for *Sambucus nigra,* the elder tree. They have also been called floral waters, herbal waters, and in Europe they are called pflansenwasser (plant water), hydrolats, hydrolato or hydrolaits. These distillate waters were highly regarded as medicine and are recently making a comeback as valuable product of distillation. Hydrosols are produced either by the essential oil industry on very large equipment or by artisan distillers on much smaller stills. Simplified, there are basically two methods of distilling in the modern age, steam distillation, where the plant material is held above the water so only steam passes through the plant material and the older method of hydro distillation, where the plant material is submerged in the water and heated. The ancient recipes used many aromatic and nonaromatic plants and they were most often hydro distilled.

Early in the 1990's, my mentor and teacher Jeanne Rose pointed me towards a text by John French, circa 1651, titled *The Art of Distillation.* This work fascinated me and was a window into the medicines of the past. This text introduced me to the terminology of the alchemists and had illustrations of the most curious looking distilling vessels. I couldn't begin to imagine how they used them.

There were many recipes of distillate waters, some of dubious ingredients. I was now thoroughly fascinated by this ancient art of distillation and threw myself into finding out as much as I could about this lost knowledge. Twenty years ago, there were few if any digitalized books, so it was difficult to find copies of the alchemist's writings. As time progressed I was able to find more and more ancient books that museums and libraries had digitalized and made available to the public. I was convinced that these books held the lost wisdom of distillers and important information on the distillate waters. Though very difficult to decipher, the books had many recipes and uses for both the aromatic and nonaromatic waters. One book in particular, *The Boke of Distyllacyon of Herbes,* published in 1527 was full of information the "Waters of Herbes". The recipes (receipts as they were called) listed over a hundred common herbs and the directions for distilling the medicinal waters. These waters were used for nearly every ailment man had in the 16th century, from ague (blindness) to worm fit (convulsions). My library is now full of both digital and facsimile copies of old herbals and cookbooks, some dating back as far as the 16th century.

DR. STEPHEN'S WATER IS MADE THUS:
*Take a gallon of Gascoigne wine; a dram each of ginger,
galganal, cinnamon, nutmeg,
grains, aniseed, fennel seeds, carroway seeds;
a handful each of sage, red mints, red
roses, thyme, pellitory, rosemary, wild thyme,
chamomile, and lavender.
Beat the spices small and bruise the herbs,
letting them macerate 12 hours, stirring them
now and then. Distil them by an alembic
or copper still with its refrigeratory. Keep the
first pint by itself, and the second by itself.
Note that the first pint will be hotter,
but the second the stronger of the ingredients.
This water is well known to comfort all the principal parts.*
(The Art of Distillation by John French 1651).

In 2014, I had the opportunity to look at old alchemy books housed at the famous Trinity Library in Dublin, Ireland. Their special collections department holds many books on alchemy and distillation. It was here that I was introduced to *Ambix*, a scholarly journal put out by the Society for the History of Alchemy and Chemistry. The library had copies of this little jewel dating back to the early 1940's. It had a wealth of information on distillation and scholarly reviews of ancient books. The journal had titles of books that I didn't even know existed. This led me to discover even more illustrations of stills and more books to request from the special collections. I was able to take notes from these old books and write down recipes that had been lost. I felt like I was on a voyage of discovery!

In 2015, I wrote a book on distilling hydrosols and touched on the subject of the evolution of the still. In this chapter, I explored how the alembic stills that are commonly used by the home distiller actually evolved and improved through the centuries. My research eventually led me to an article on "the world's oldest perfume factory" and the work of Dr. Belgiorno. Reading about the excavation at Pyrgos was the information I was looking for; it was her work that inspired me to dig even deeper into the history of these waters and distillation. Imagine making medicines and perfumes 4000 years ago! The alembic still Belgiorno commissioned for her experimental archaeology was the inspiration for me to explore how the stills had evolved over time. Many of us who distil at home prefer the older style of stills, such as the classic copper alembic still.

I started distilling on what is called a pot still, which consists of a pot, and onion shaped hat and a water bath that contains the condensing coil; the condensing coil being a fairly modern invention.

In the United States, the only hydrosols available twenty years ago were often a by-product of the essential oil industry. This both limited the variety and quality of the hydrosols. It was common to find rose water, neroli water, lavender hydrosol and perhaps a few more. These were essentially the waste product from the distillation of plant material to recover the volatile components of the plants (the essential oil). These hydrosols were used mostly as room sprays and not regarded as a therapeutic product. Other countries have had a long history hydrosol, especially the rose and neroli waters; they have been in cooking, medicine, beautification and more for centuries, if not longer. With the rise of popularity of hydrosols, it is now quite easy to find many varieties of hydrosols, both from aromatic (essential oil bearing plants) and nonaromatic plants.

Many aromatherapists and herbalists are taking up the craft of distilling and producing some of high quality distillate waters.

It is once again common to use hydrosols on a daily basis. The uses are nearly endless. In herbal and aromatherapy practices you may see practitioners using the hydrosols as room sprays, both for deodorizing and for energy clearing; perhaps between clients. It is common for an aromatherapist to use hydrosols as the base in their lotions and creams they make for clients, adding an extra level of therapeutics. Herbalists may use the hydrosol as the water for a compress or poultice, adding it to the herbs. Hydrosols can be used in wound care and in first aid. Adding the distillate waters to a foot bath or hand bath is a perfect addition to a hydrotherapy treatment.

Hydrosols have also found their way into the kitchen. Rose and neroli water have a long history of culinary uses. More recently hydrosols are used in ice cubes for summer drinks; peppermint ice cubes in your ice tea is very refreshing. Basil hydrosol is an excellent choice as the base for sauces and creams. Rosemary and sage are great for spritzing on vegetables and meat for flavour during cooking. Hydrosols are much easier to use than their essential oil counterparts and do not overwhelm the taste buds. Many aromatic hydrosols have been included in the new trend of designer cocktails, where the distillate waters are used to flavour spirits.

In July of 2017 I had the pleasure of speaking at the world's first congress on hydrosols, *Aqua Aromatica*. It was held at a beautiful garden centre, Staudengärnerei Gaissmayer in Illertissen, Germany.

The conference took place at the Museum of Garden Culture, a very fitting venue for hosting a conference on the Waters of Distillation. It was at this event that I was able to finally meet Dr. Belgiorno in person. I had been following her work for a number of years. Our hostess Susanne Fischer-Rizzi, an experienced distiller, brought together experts from across the globe. Her work entitled, *Opus Mulierum – The lost art of women*, was a look back at the women alchemists of the millennia. Fischer-Rizzi focused on thirteen women alchemists. Her Opus starts with Aphrodite and works its way through history up to Grace Firth, a 21st century alchemist.

Aqua Aromatica was a perfect blend of both the science and the mysteries that these hydrosols hold. There were lectures and workshops on distillation, veterinary work with hydrosols, hospice care with hydrosols, cooking with hydrosols and much more.

Berthold Heusel had a presentation that showed photos of hydrosols under a dark field microscope. Dr. Belgiorno presented her work on the history of distillation and the evolution of the alembic stills.

Her lecture added depth to the *Opus Mulierum*, as her discovery of the world's oldest still was discovered at the Pyrgos site; Pyrgos is on the island of Cyprus, the birthplace of Aphrodite.

Dr. Belgiorno brought a replica of the still that was discovered at Pyrgos, part of her experimental archaeology, whereby one test hypotheses by trying to replicate equipment and perform tasks that ancient cultures may have used. Our conversations throughout the event focused on stills and distillation. Her work with experimental archaeology, was also a topic of interest. It is through this collaboration of ideas and research that the idea for this book was born; to trace the evolution of distillation throughout the ages. It is my hope that our partnership will include distilling together, using the replicated stills to produce the recipes of old.

Ann Harman

ann@circlehinstitute.com
www.circlehinstitute.com

Behind distillation

I. Technology.

'And those who were seen dancing were thought to be insane by those who could not hear the music': Friedrich Nietzsche, 1883

Distillation is the simplest method to separate organic and inorganic substances after vaporization, cooling, condensation, or sublimation.

It is so simple and brilliant that research into when, where and who discovered this scientific process started long ago. We do not have any straight description of it before the famous report of Aristoteles. But if we pay attention to its functioning, diverting our attention from the apparatus, we can frame the discovery in a specific time after the appearance of a series of objects linked in some way to the same purpose and use.

The scope was to take something wrapped in something else to possess it and create somewhat of different, taking power over nature.

Distillation is deeply linked with the knowledge of the existence of different components in natural organic and inorganic material.

The awareness of the presence of different substances and elements in the surrounding world was a gradual progression, which aroused philosophical reflections addressed to understand and take advantage of the most secret laws of life. Before the philosophical implications, we can presume that a very long period of study and experimentation preceded the invention of the first devices to separate substances.

The key of research is that if an alembic exists, the beginning of its knowledge must have been a long path of experience addressed to understand what there is inside organic and inorganic material and study its properties.

So, we must point our attention to the first methodologies utilized to separate the component of rocks, fruits, or flowers to take its colour, oil, or scent[1]. If we go back in time we find most of the knowledge based on the evolution of the Pyro technology, the art of using the fire.

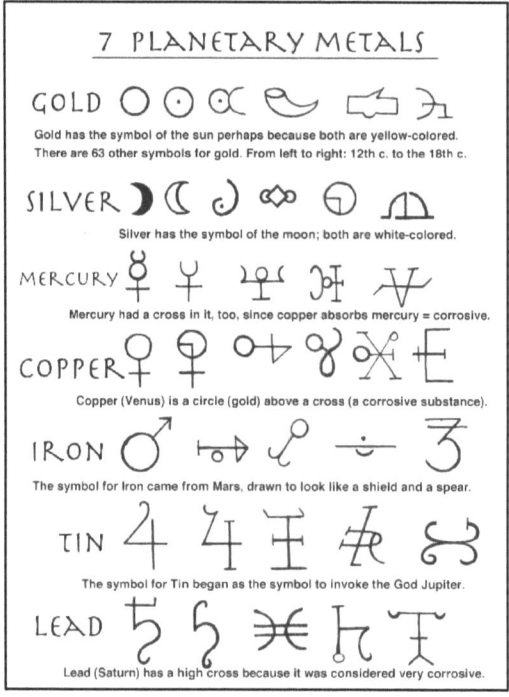

Fig.1: Table of the Seven Planetary Metals.

Fire separates and fire joins the elements. The simple fact that in Mesopotamia the Babylonians identified metals with planets (Fig.1) give us the certainty that they acknowledged the differences: Gold/Sun, Silver/Moon, Lead/Saturn, Electrum/Jupiter, Iron/Mars, Copper/Venus,

---

[1] Paul T. Keyser S. R. James, "Hominid Use of Fire in the Lower and Middle Pleistocene: A Review of the Evidence," Current Anthropology 30 (1989) 1-26; which takes us back, to the Palaeolithic Middle Pleistocene of 200,000 years ago—and the mastery of fire. J. Forbes, Studies in Ancient Technology (= SAT) VI (Leiden 1948).

Tin/Jupiter. In the long history of metallurgy, we find that man discovered first how to remove metal from the rock with smelting (Fig. 2) and after many years there developed a possibility to make alloys inventing new metals with different characteristics that could facilitate the making of objects and their aspect.

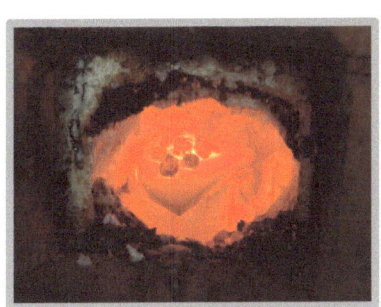 

Fig. 2: Fire separates and fire joins before and after a crucible.

The process is based on the same concept, that of the different nature and composition of each rock. The problem was essential to know the difference of temperature you must reach for separating each element, the same that in turn melt at a different temperature, so that every metal is a distinctive individual which reacts in a dissimilar manner when it is submitted to the fire. The funny thing is that we are speaking about something that happened in the prehistory, meanwhile the story of alchemy tells us that we must look at the Greek philosophers to find traces of knowledge of singular elements.

Therefore, if we read the famous Egyptian medical papyri, some of which belonging to the beginning of the 2nd millennium BC, recording recipes in use of metallurgy from centuries back, we find how wrong our assumptions have been[2].

---

[2] Most of these recipes report the use of distinct elements, proving the knowledge of different substances and their possible use to compose specific products. Papyrus of

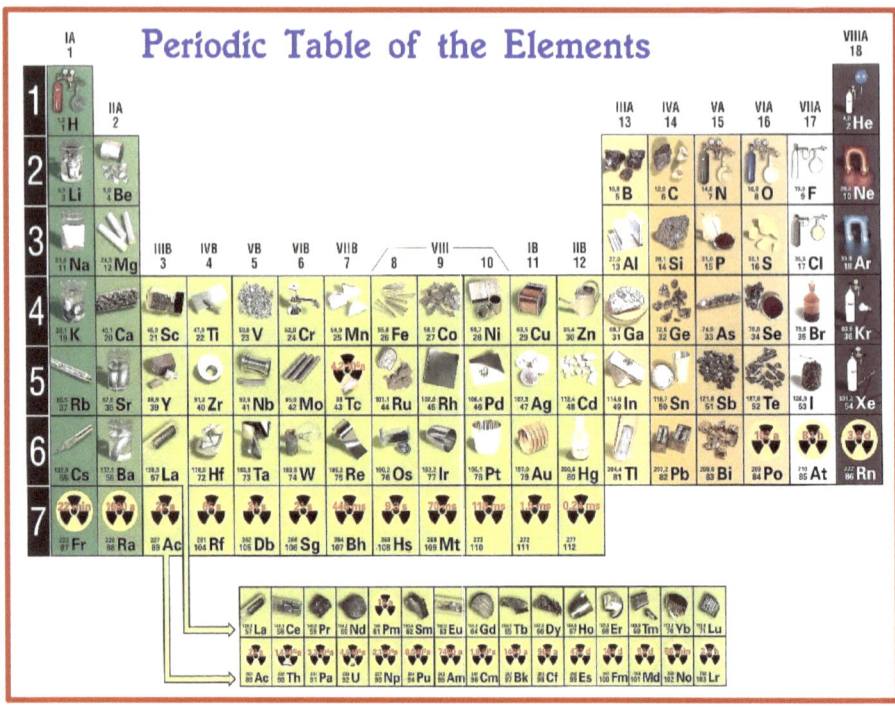

Fig. 3: Periodic Table of the Elements including metalloids.

Notwithstanding this, in the history of chemistry we find that the properties and differences between metals and metalloids have been discovered in the 19th century (Fig. 3), many centuries after the collapsing of the Roman Empire, the firing of the Alexandria library[3] and the destruction of Bagdad university, which resulted in the complete loss of the scientific works, treaties and compendiums of the most important philosophers and mathematicians of the Hellenistic and Roman periods,

---

Leyden X 23, mentions arsenic (or antimony?) plating as a way of producing silver from copper:

[3] In 389 A.D. the Serapion of Alexandria and its library was destroyed under an edict of Theodosius calling for the destruction of all pagan temples within the Empire. In the same year, Zeno, Emperor of the East, closed the important school at Edessa and its Nestorian teachers were banished, finding refuge in Asia. The University/Museum of Alexandria, survived until 415 when a Christians riots killed the last scholars and teachers of Alexandrian school including Hypatia (370 - 415).
 http://www.astr.ua.edu/4000ws/Hypatia.htmlWS/HYPATIA.html.

circulating in all the territories conquered by Alexander the Great and Rome. The descendants of the barbarian hordes in Italy plundered and set on fire every place that could still preserve ancient manuscripts that maintained centuries, if not millennia, of scientific knowledge of the Roman Empire. Only the Arab world, unified by one language spread throughout the Middle East, North Africa, the Mediterranean regions, and territories occupied by the Ottoman Empire, thanks to the Koran, managed to retain some of that immense knowledge.

Fig. 4: The laboratory of Merlin in "The sword in the stone" film by Walt Disney 1963.

While the world belonging to the former Latin and Greek languages dipped in almost total illiteracy. The rare erudite Europeans who had the fortune to study in one of the monasteries that preserved copies of the fragments survived after the immense disaster were forced to retrace the long journey that led to knowledge.

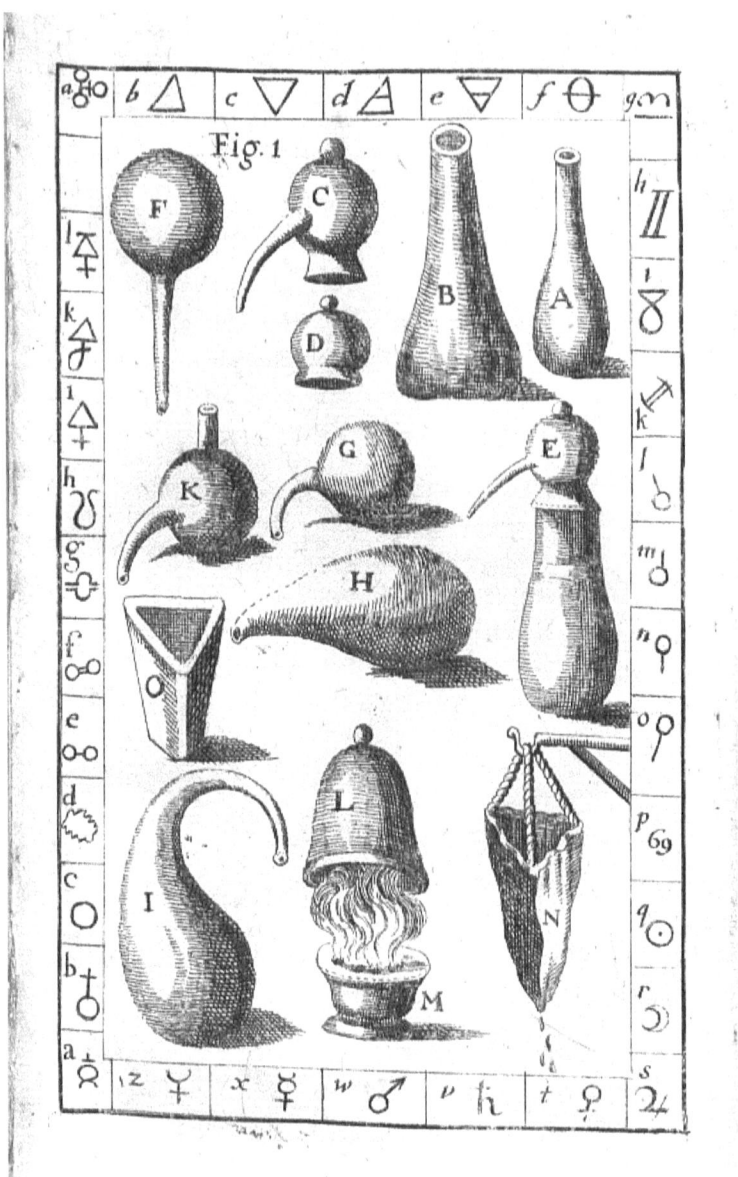

Fig. 5: Alchemical apparatuses. Carlo Lancillotti, *Nuova guida alla chimica, che per suo mezzo conduce gli affetionati alle operazioni sopra ogni corpo misto animale, minerale ò vegetabile. Dichiarando come estraggono i loro sali, essenzi, magisterii, mercurii etc. con il modo di fare varii colori & altri rari secreti. In quest'ultima impressione ampliata di nuove aggiunte & figure etc, et in tre parti divisa.* Venetia 1681: (L + M) is an Aludel.

Considered more magicians than scientists these scholars belong to the class of the Philosophers/ Alchemists, and their science still today it is not considered with all the respect that is due (Fig. 4). The abyss between knowledge and complete ignorance led to regard the alchemical laboratories little more than the cave of the magician composing potions which gave transformations and incredible powers.

Considering what is reported about pre-modern scientific texts it appears that the situation has not changed much after the Renaissance.

Reading these texts, it seems that before Empedocles, Plato, Leucippus and Aristoteles[4] the people did not know the difference between simple and composed materials. We have to arrive at Paracelsus 16th century to find the principles of how the bodies are made, and to Albertus Magnus (1250) to find metalloids as Arsenic evaluated as distinct elements; when for instance Arsenic was not only known since prehistory, but also used as an individual ingredient to make medicines and metal alloys since the 3rd millennium BC, as we can see in the masterpieces of jewellery of the Tutankhamun treasure, made with iron oxides and arsenic to create the famous purple gold[5]. Naturally occurring arsenic is extremely rare and to get it, it is necessary to submit the arsenical sulphides[6], which are the most common minerals containing arsenic, to a reduction process that involves

---

[4] J. E. Bolzan 1976: Chemical Combination According to Aristotle, Ambix 23: 134-44.
[5] R. W. Wood, "The Purple Gold of Tutankhamun," JEA 20 (1934) 62-66, Pl. XI. 63; C. S. Smith, "An Examination of the Arsenic-Rich Coating on a Bronze Bull from Horoztepe," in Application of Science in Examination of Works of Art, ed. W. J. Young.; C. G. Fink and A. H. Kopp, "Ancient Antimony Plating on Copper Objects," Met. Mus. Studies 4 (1933) 163-67.
[6] Arsenic is a metalloid, naturally combined with other metals, sulphur and oxygen, different in colour: Realgar (AsS) red, Orpiment (As2S3) yellow, Arsenolite (As2O3) white and Arsenopyrite (FeAsS) grey. The word arsenic is derived from the Persian *zarnikh* and Syriac *zarniqa*, later transformed by Greeks as *arsenikon,* which means "male". In the 4th century BC, Hippocrates and Theophrastus knew the medical and poisoning properties of arsenic. At the time, both Realgar and Orpiment were used to treat ulcers and abscesses not only for cosmetic purposes.

sublimation in an Aludel, an apparatus commonly named *the blind alembic*[7].

The device (Fig. 5) mainly attends to sublimate mercury (cinnabar), sulphur, and arsenic sulphides (Realgar and orpiment). It is made of glass or clay and consists of two pots or tubes fitted together. The mineral is put in the lower vessel covered and sealed by the upper pot and the whole is put on the fire (Fig.6).

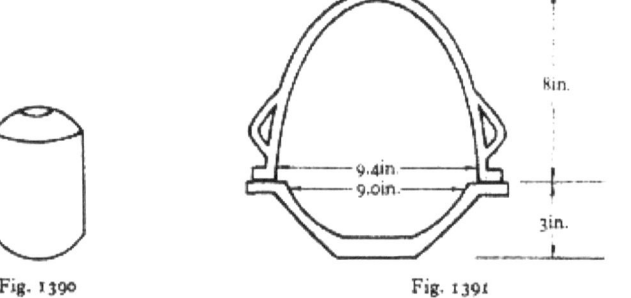

Fig. 6: Aludel working, from Needham 1980 p. 22.

---

[7]M. Berthelot 1887 Collection Des Anciens Alchimistes Grecs Fig. 45, Bibliotheca Chemica de Manget 540, t. I, fig. 2; Genève, 1702; Carlo Lancillotti: 1681, Nuova guida alla chimica, che per suo mezzo conduce gl'affetionati alle operazioni sopra ogni corpo misto animale, minerale ò vegetabile... Venetia.

The ascending vapour gets to the upper tube without oxygen cooling and sublimating in solid state the substance request (mercury, sulphur and arsenic).[8] Dioscurides (Diosc. V:95) and Pliny the elder (Naturalis Historiae XXXIII:123) reported the sublimation of mercury in the first century A.D, when mercury was mainly used for refining gold and silver[9].

The difference is that in the same period arsenic had already been used for many centuries by metal alloys and pharmaceutical compositions.

This suggests sublimation was a technology known for many centuries. Both the metalloids and their natural sulphides have been the substance around which much of medieval alchemy evolved in the search for the famous philosopher's stone. Of the Hellenistic and Roman periods, we do not have any device that has survived, as terracotta distillers for sublimation or kitchen pots seldom superimposed, since they were of little value and once worn they were thrown away, while the fragments of glass specimens were melt again to make new objects. So, during the centuries many forms of devices have disappeared completely from memory.

Today, after the recovering of many texts saved and transcribed by the Arabs and the possibility to translate the hieroglyphics of the Egyptian papyri and inscriptions, Alchemy is regarded with different eyes and we recognise its role in the history of science.

* * *

---

[8] Marcellin Berthelot (1893), *La chimie au moyen âge*, **1**, Imprimerie nationale, pp. 109, 149–150, 170

[9] A.R. Butler, J. Needham, An Experimental Comparison of the East Asian, Hellenistic and Indian (Gandharan) Stills in Relation to the Distillation of Ethanol and Acetic Acid, "Ambix" XXVII (1980) 69-76.

Now I have introduced the historical scenario in which many scholars think was the beginning of distillation/sublimation, wrongly considered an Arab invention, to carry on laboratory experiments addressed on changing and replicating the natural composition of mineral and organic material to create new substances.

What will follow is a brief compendium of the written documentation, which can help in recognising the evidence brought to the light by the Archaeological investigations which started around the beginning of 1800.

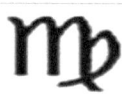

II. Ancient texts.

With a rapid bird's eye on the ancient written texts and their surviving, we can find the reasons of the incorrect attribution of distillation to the Arabs. The news we have about the most ancient knowledge which left written texts include the Chinese herbal treaty *Herbarium*, which is believed to have been written for a divine inspiration by the "Red Emperor" Shen Nung in the third millennium BC (2838-2698 BC). This famous Herbarium, known under the name of *Pen Ts' ao Ching* (Latin *Shen Nung Materia medica,* or the great Herbarium), illustrates and describes many medicinal plants and 237 herbal prescriptions, using dozens of different plants, including Ephedra (Ephedra sp.), Rhubarb (Rhubarb) and Opium (*Papaver somniferous*).

In India, we find the four books of Ayurveda, word meaning knowledge of the life (Ayur =life and Veda=knowledge), conserving the oldest testimonies about the pharmaceutical properties of plants[10].

The oldest, the Rig-Veda dates to 3000/4500 before present, while the complete version dates to 2000 BC circa. In that, also the religious hymns describe surgical operations and formulas for composing medicines using 67 herbs.

During 1600 BC the famous Egyptian Papyrus was also discovered by George Ebers at Luxor. In almost 20 meters in length the document describes more than a millennium of Pharaonic medicine and lists 876

---

[10] Ramchandra Narayan Dandekar 2005. In, *Encyclopaedia of Religion*, Mac Millaned vol. XIV, 9550, New York.

herbal formulas based on about five hundred plants, of which about a third are still used in modern pharmacological compositions (Fig.7).

Fig.7: Page of Ebers Papyrus, University library Lipsia.

In Mesopotamia, we have Akkadian cuneiform texts of the 3rd and 2nd millennium BC, which contain lists of ingredients and recipes for pharmaceutical compounds and cosmetics. Some texts published by scholar Martin Levey constitute today the earliest documentation of the ancient Sumerian Pharmacy and knowledge of distillation[11].

Centuries after the Egyptian papyri and the Akkadian texts, the Mycenaean linear B tablets from the second half of the second millennium BC record trades of fragrant oils and spices between the Mediterranean

---

[11] A Group of Akkadian Texts on Perfumery" in M. Levey 1960. Early Muslim Chemistry: its debt to Ancient Babylonia, in *Chymia*, Annual Studies in the History of Chemistry, University of Pennsylvania Press, H.M. Leicester ed. Vol.6, Philadelphia; M. Levey 1955. Evidences of ancient distillation, sublimation and extraction in Mesopotamia, in *Centaurus*, 22-33; Early Arabic Pharmacology: An Introduction Based on Ancient and Medieval Sources, Leiden 1973.

countries, including Cyprus, and mention some of the most common plants used to compose the fragrances[12] (Fig. 8).

Fig. 8: KN FH371 Linear B tablet (didactic replica).

The first classification of about 300 species of medicinal plants is due to Hippocrates of Kos (460-377 BC about), one of the most famous Greek physicists (Fig.10), while the oldest systematic pharmaceutical treatise of botany *De Historia Plantarum*, was written by the Aristotelian Theophrastus (Eresos, Lesbos 372-287 BC). Aristotle (384—322 BC) in Meteorology affirms "sea water can be made drinkable by vaporisation; other liquids behave in the same way". Nicander (183—135 BC) of Colophon, a Greek poet and physician, mentions a method of extraction of perfumes from plants[13] that reminds us of distillation.

A few centurics later in the 1st century AD, Dioscurides Pedanius from Anazarba in Cilicia 1st cent. AD enriched the Hippocrates' work, writing a famous *treatise* written in Greek that was translated into Latin only in XV century with the title of *De Materia Medica*, listing more than 500

---

[12] C. Wright Shelmerdine 1985. *The perfume Industry of Mycenaean Pylos*, Goteborg: P. Astrom Forlag.
[13] Gorreus J. 1549: *Nicandri Colophonii Alexipharmaca. Io. Gorraeo Parisiensi medico interprete. Eiusdem interpretis in Alexipharmaca praefatio, omnem de uenenis disputationem summatim complectens, & annotationes*. Parisiis, apud Vascosanum via Iacobaea, ad insigne Fontis; Brenning M. 1904: Nikanders Theriaka und Alexipharmaka. Allgemeine medizinische Central-Zeitung, 73: 112–114, 132–134, 327–330, 346–349, 368–371 and 387–390.

substances including spices, minerals, plants, and animals useful to make pharmaceutical remedies and perfumes. After Pedanius, many scholars produced similar works, however, for most of them we know only the name of their treaty and a few pages. Among the most important alchemist we find Apollonius of Cyprus, pharmacist of *Citium* (Kition = Larnaca, called "Mys" (1st cent. BC), mentioned by the young Andromacho, Galen, and Oribasius), who writes *"De unguentum",* where he affirms that the best grape scent is that of Cyprus and mentions the excellence of the fragrance produced by Cypriot Henna (or Kypros), second only to the Egyptian (Athenaeus: Deipnosophistis, 38/688).

Fig. 9: Saint Hippolytus, Fresco of XI c. in the Church of St. George at Staro Nagoričane, Macedonia.

Many scholars agree that the first recorded wine distilling formula for making the special beverage to celebrate Dionysian festivals, belongs to Anaxilaus of Thessaly, who was ousted from Rome in 28 BC for honing enchantment. Anaxilaus' recipe is supposedly reported by Saint Hippolytus, presbyter of Rome 200 AD (Fig.9), in the book written in Greek "Philosophoumena" Liber IV- cap. 31, Latin version "Refutatio omnium haeresium"[14]. In the 1st cent. AD, Aulus Cornelius Celsius wrote "*De artibus*" a treatise on the entire medical knowledge of the time, which included and reported the medicinal properties of plants.

Fig. 10: Hippocrates and Galeno, crypt of Anagni Cathedral.

However, the most important treatise of the Greek-Roman period remains the vast compendium of Pliny the elder, famous for having lost his life to watch from the sea the Vesuvius eruption that destroyed Pompeii and Herculaneum in 79 AD. His *Naturalis Historia* is the only one that describes the recipes and botanical notes taken directly from Theophrastus

---

[14] Hyppolytus, "*Philosophoumena*" Liber IV- cap. 31, Latin version "*Refutatio omnium haeresium*", translated by Hermann Diels Doxographi Graeci, 306, Berlin, 1879.

and Dioscurides, suggesting he was aware of distilled spirits when in the liber XIV, ch. 12 and ch. 22 he says: " Oh! Wondrous craft of the vices! by some mode or other it was discovered that water itself might be made to inebriate." The written research by Galen of Pergamum (129-216 AD), a physicist at the Court of the emperors Marcus Aurelius, Commodus, and Septimius Severus, are mainly based on the writings of Hippocrates (Fig. 10). Even Synesius (373-414) describes the alchemical distillation in his treatise "*The true book about the philosopher's stone* (or stone of the philosophers: *lapis philosophorum*, of Doctor Synesius Greek Abbot: translation: Paris 1611. Precise descriptions of Egyptian alchemical knowledge and of making fragrances and pharmacological remedies in the late Imperial period are reported in the writings of Zosimos of Panopolis, a (pseudo) Democritean alchemist of III-IV c. AD (Fig. 11).

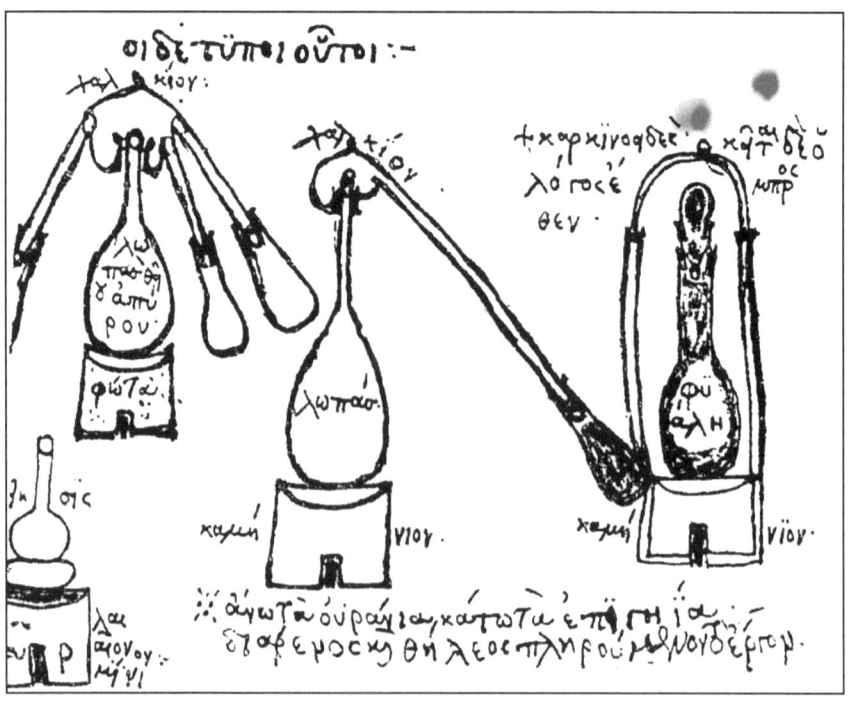

Fig. 11: Apparatus for distillation of Maria the Jewesh, by Zosimos, M. Berchelot, *Collection des Anciens Alchemists Grecs,* Paris 1887-1888.

The book focuses on the analysis of the four main components that make up the world: fire, air, water, and soil. It includes a reasoned analysis on the relationship between high temperature and motion, within which, in an extremely precise manner the writer explains what occurs during the distillation, when vapour emerges and rises to gravity: *"the movement is due to the warmth since through heat each element becomes active"*. His work, *The keys of wisdom,* (*Chemeutikà*) on perfumes and pharmaceutical remedies is located within an Arabic manuscript in 1100 (published in 1800) of the Kurdish scholar Mu'ayyad al-Din Abu Isma'il al-Husayn Ibn Ali al-Tughra'I (1061-1121)[15]. Many students consider him the famous alchemist "Artephius", author of the treatise "The secret book of Artephius" that reports many recipes and investigations about the elixir of long life and the *philosopher's stone*.

Fig. 12: Saint'Isidore of Seville, présentant *"Défense de la foi catholique"* à sa soeur Florentine Bnf, Manuscript, Latin 13396 fol.iv.

---

[15] H.S. El Khadem 1996. A Translation of a Zosimos Text in an Arabic Alchemy Book, in *Journal of the Washington Academy of Sciences* vol.84, 168-178.

In the VI century Alexander of Tralles, brother of the architect who had built Santa Sophia in Constantinople, wrote a pharmaceutical compendium with the name of "*De arte medicinae*", containing the recipes of healing perfumes and pills, including strong fragrances such as Myrrh, Incense and Saffron. The last scholar of the ancient world that dealt with medicines and perfumes is the bishop Saint Isidore of Seville (560-636) (Fig. 12), which, after request of Braulione of Zaragoza, wrote the *Etymologiae*, the first Encyclopaedic history of Science composed of 20 books and 443 chapters. After the birth of the Islamic religion, in the seventh century (Mohammed was born around 570) the herbal knowledge of the ancient capital Byzantium was collected from the Arab.

Fig.13: The Medicine of the Prophet.

Mohammed himself, a native of the tribe of Quraysh, was a seller of perfumes and spices and has left many short letters, comments, and recipes, later collected in 1350 by the renowned theologian Ibn Qayyim al-Jawziyya in a famous work entitled "*The medicine of the prophet*" (Fig. 13). Under the government of the Abbasid Caliphs, between 750 and 1258 some Christian scholars, including John of Mesue (the old) and Serapion (the old), translated Greek and Latin compendia into Arabic. After the expulsion for heresy of the patriarch Nestor from Constantinople (431 AD), a school of medicine and science was established in the Iranian Khorestan (Fig.14), where Nestorian monks translated into Arabic the books of Dioscurides, Galen and other scientists, saving some of their works, but transferring the ancient knowledge in the Arab culture and tradition.

Fig. 14: Metallurgy and distillation in the same room. Khorestan, Iran XIX c.

Toward the VIII-IX century, three schools of Alchemy were founded. The first was the Iran-Mesopotamic school with the famous scientists "Jabir" (Abu Musa Jabir ibn Hayyan al azdi born in Tus in Iran in 721, died in Kufa Iraq, in 815), "al Razi" (Abu Bakr Mohammad ibn Zakariya al Razi born at Ray 864-930) and "Avicenna" (Abū Alī al-Ḥusayn ibn ʿAbd Allāh ibn Sīnā, born at Balkh in 980, died at Hamadan in 1037).

The second was the school of Andalusia in Spain, represented by Abulcasis Al-Zahr āwī (936-1013), the author of the treaty of surgery Kitab al-Tassif (inspired by Paul of Aegina), the physician-surgeon Avenzoar (Abd al-Malik ibn Zuhr 1090-1162 (Fig.15) and by his disciple Averroës, philosopher and physician, famous for his philosophical commentaries on Aristotle.

Fig. 15: Abd al-Malik Ibn Zuhr al-Ishbili, Avenzoar Siviglia.

The third, the Egyptian school at Cairo mainly represented by Ibn- El-Baitar (Benalmadena Spain 1197 - Damascus 1248), author of "Diami El Marfridat", alphabetic treaty of herbs, animals, and minerals with annotations on their uses and properties.

Thanks to their lists of plants, treatises of medicine and summaries of formulas, the ancient Mediterranean wisdom has been maintained.

The first cosmetologist or doctor in cosmetics was, however, Abu'al-Qassim Al Zahrawil or Abulcassis of Cordova (1100) who wrote the "Encyclopaedia Al-Tasreef" in 30 volumes, reporting an exact description of the apparatus to distil wine and roses. In its chapter 19, we find wide research on cosmetics of that time. His treaty translated into Latin, became the Bible of western cosmetics for a very long period. Al-Zahrawil considers cosmetics a branch of medicine, calling it "*Medicine of beauty*" (Adwiyat al-Zinah). His disposition toward perfumes led him to include perfumes and incense in the recipes of cosmetics and medicines.

Among his recipes, there are also prescriptions on how to prepare solid soap, lipsticks, and solid ointment rolled and pressed into special moulds, used as deodorant sticks, creating the antecedents of the products used today all around the world.

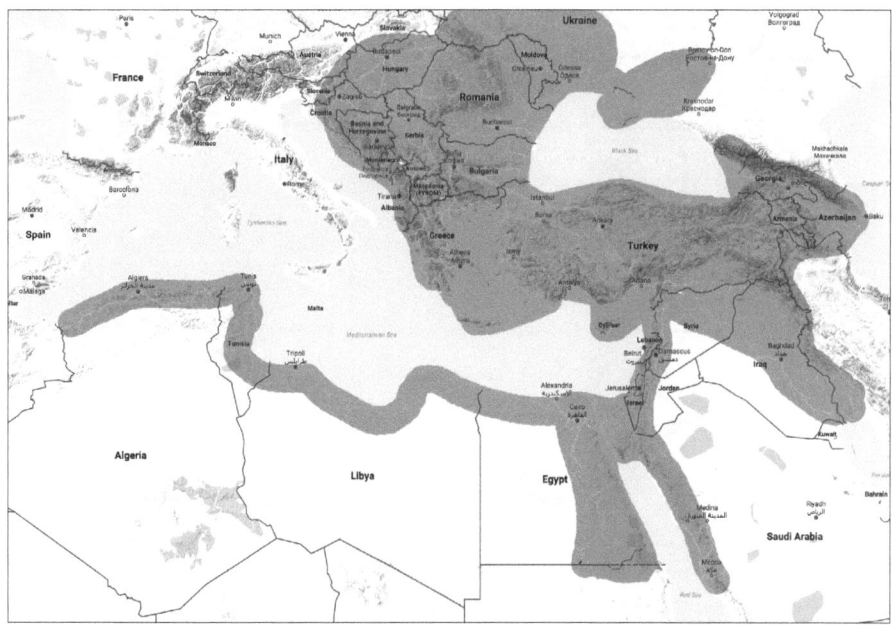

Fig. 16: Maximum Ottoman Empire expansion.

During the VIII century, the Caliph Al-Manzur (Abū Jaʿfar ʿAbd Allāh ibn Muḥammad al-Manṣūr, Arabic ابو جعفر عبدالله ابنحمد المنصور Humayma ca. 712 - Baghdad 775), the founder of Islàmic Baghdad with its famous rounded citadel, created a pharmaceutical workshop specialized in perfumes and vegetable drugs (including Anise, Enula, Benzoin, Beth-el, Borage, Caoutchouc, Colochintha, cinnamon, Fumaria, Nut Vomica, Saffron, nails of Carnatia, Manna, Nutmeg, White Poppy, Pyrethrum, Rhubarb, Rosemary, Rose, Sandal and Marijuana). Considering the activity and the importance of the three schools, it is assumed that between the VIII and the XII century, the Arab culture, that made treasure of Koran teachings and language, preserved, and put forward all the information unified by Roman Empire expansion.

Therefore, we can say with good reason that in the centuries before the beginning of the second millennium, the medical and pharmaceutical science, including the art of perfumery, was conducted in Arabic (Fig.16).

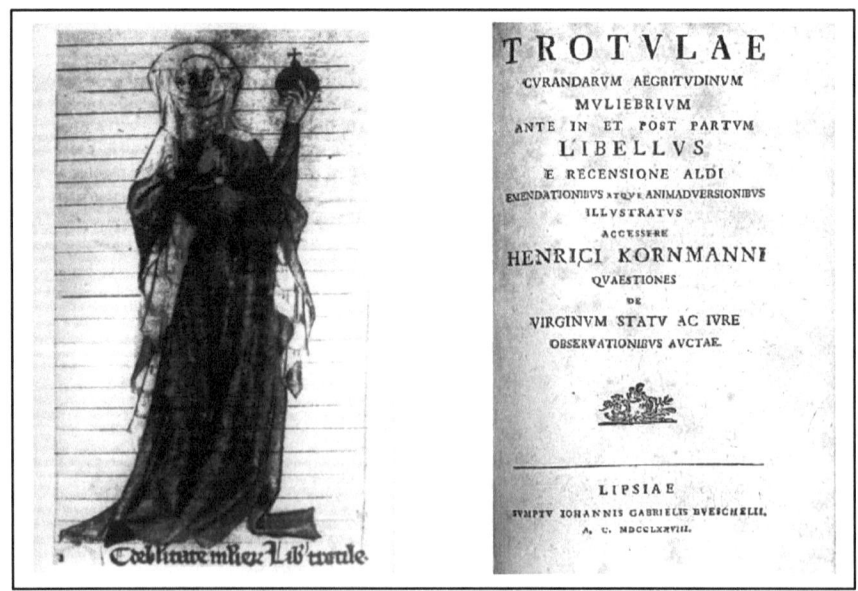

Fig. 17: A Medieval portrait of Trotula de Ruggiero and her book.

However, even if the history of alchemy assigns to the Arabs the discovery of alcohol, obtained by distilling wine, it seems that the first experimentation that substituted alcohol for oil as vehicle of fragrant essences was made in Italy. In fact, the Superior Institute of Sciences of Salerno was the first that under Gisulf II (1030-1091) admitted women in the course in medicine, becoming responsible for an epochal turning.

In its laboratory, directed in 1050 by a woman, doctor Trotula de Ruggiero (belonging to a noble and rich Salerno family), famous for her exceptional teaching skills, alcohol first replaced oil as an excipient for perfume (Fig. 17). The event is reported in detail in the manuscripts of that time. However, the first "modern" perfume in alcoholic solution was prepared in Hungary in 1370 by a monk expert of chemistry.

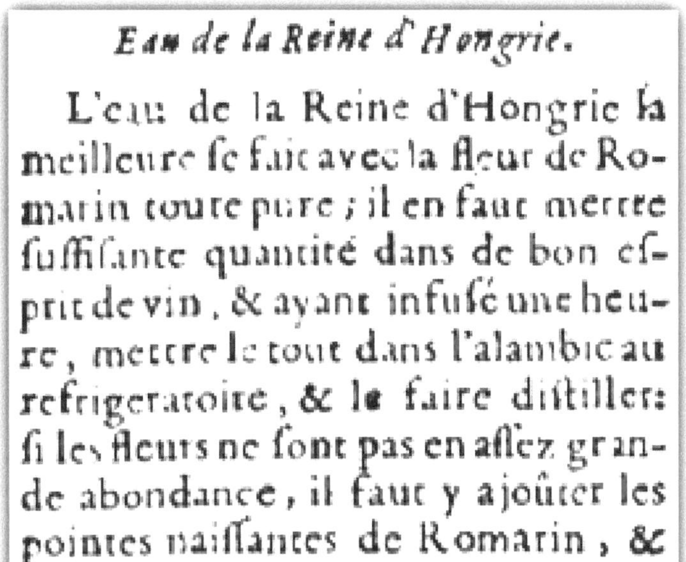

Eau de la Reine d'Hongrie.

L'eau de la Reine d'Hongrie la meilleure se fait avec la fleur de Romarin toute pure; il en faut mettre suffisante quantité dans de bon esprit de vin, & ayant infusé une heure, mettre le tout dans l'alambic au refrigeratoire, & le faire distiller: si les fleurs ne sont pas en assez grande abondance, il faut y ajoûter les pointes naissantes de Romarin, & elle n'en sera pas moins bonne.

Fig. 18: The "Hungarian water" recipe: *"Eau de Cologne"*. *http://p9.storage.canalblog.com/97/21/558745/45898530.*

The fragrance called *Eau de Hongrie* ("Hungarian Water") was an extract of Rosemary, Thyme, and Lavender. Saint Elizabeth of Thuringia, Queen of Hungary, the "princess of the poor", created the first (Fig. 18).

The composition was based on Rosemary macerated in alcohol, with the addition of Lavender, Thistle, Bergamot, Amber and Jasmine. In 1979, the Maison Fragonard (Grasse) has recreated the "Eau de Hongrie", according to its original formula, and it is still in production in Hungary

III. Prehistory

Now, we pass to analyse the subject from the archaeological point of view, starting from prehistory.

The knowledge of how to separate the elements is really at the beginning of the History of Science, and it is deeply linked to the intellectual progress and cultural development of the ancient civilizations.

Still today we can find the difference between countries, which since prehistory have possessed a high technological knowledge and people who do not, despite the globalization of information through net. To find traces of this ancient awareness, before writing documentation, we should find evidence of the first attempts to use different elements to produce something of new: as a colour, a taste, or a scent including chosen components. In a few words, a special recipient arranged not to separate, but to mix different substances among them.

There is a clay object that appears around the 4th millennium BC in Mesopotamia and later in the Near East, Egypt, and Cyprus which we could take as a symbol of this new knowledge and awareness.

It is the so called "kernos", a ring "vase" with some holed bowls positioned on the body through which you can pour inside the ring vase different ingredients[16]. The miracle of their union takes place out of your sight in a closed and magical environment. However, the Cypriot

---

[16] Bignasca A.M. 2000: *I kernoi circolari in Oriente e in Occidente. Strumenti di culto e immagini cosmiche*, Universitätsverlag Freibueg Schweiz Vandenhoeck & Ruprecht Göttingen.

specimens are not the most ancient. We must go back to Mesopotamia to find the oldest, which date back to the late 5th millennium BC.

Fig. 19 a-b; Fig 20 a-b; Early Bronze age kernoi,
St. Barnaba Monastery Museum, Northern Cyprus.

The two devices from Cyprus (Fig. 19a-b; and Fig. 20 a-b) date back to the late 3rd Millennium BC, and are made using standard bowls of everyday use applied to the ring vase. The holes in the bottom of the bowls show clearly the intention to mix in the vacuum ring vase different liquid substances. The first is one of the first version standing on three feet, originally holding a cover for each bowl (one preserved). The presence of the covers suggests that the liquid was poured until it reached the rims of the bowls, and then left for a precise time before the final use. This is the case for which the Archaeometry analyses of the remains inside the ring vase could give valuable information about the destination of such famous objects. Some *kernoi* have been found near temples, not in direct connection with cult ceremonies, most have been found in tombs such as in Cyprus, and we can suppose that their use was more apotropaic and magic than religious. However, if they testify to an acquired knowledge, we should consider them a prehistoric philosophical thought. Pottery, metallurgy, and glass making are important milestones of human progress.

All arts based on the perfect use and knowledge of specific elements, masterfully separated using fire and water then melted together again, using fire to create useful objects and instruments. Without them, we would not be talking about distillation. Of course, the story began with the invention of pottery.

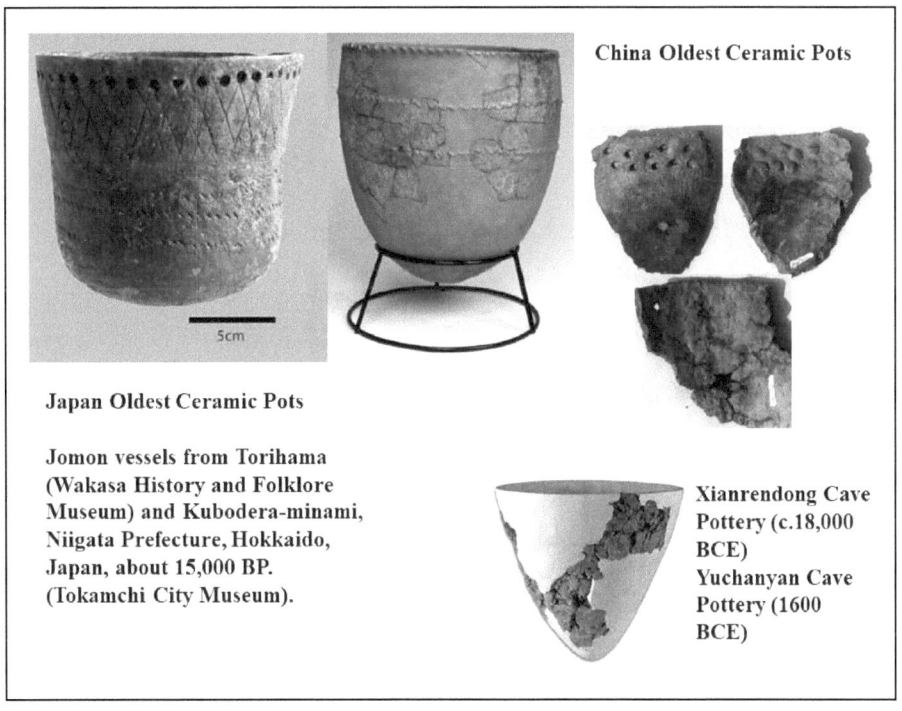

Fig. 21: Some of the oldest ceramics in the world found in China and Japan.

It is commonly accepted that the first shapes of pots are simple bowls probably invented in China or Japan between the 13th or 16th millennia BC, many centuries before the invention of metals and glass, which are today the main material used to still (Fig. 21).

Therefore, we must turn our attention to the primary simple shapes of clay pots to find the first rude devices to separate substances. It is quite difficult that in antiquity, people discovered distillation trying to emulate the action of the sun producing steam from heating water and organic material, which going up in the colder atmosphere transforms it before in clouds and then in water. It is much more likely that they gradually came to understand the function of the distillation during the cooking of food through the observation of liquid condensation under the lids of the pots[17].

Considering that the first covers were probably rounded stones or simple bowls positioned over the mouth of the pot, we can find the starting point which attracted the attention of a man/woman, who was present during cooking. After observing the boiling of the liquid inside the pot, he found that some liquid was dropping from the lid and simply he collected it in a bowl tasting the result. Without knowing the importance of the action, that person had begun a path of knowledge that would take them through many experiences in discovering the different composition of many substances.

Another crucial step was the observation and use of further natural phenomena such as the division of the organic elements through fermentation and maceration. In this circumstance, the separator and aggregating factor is water, present in high percentage in fruits and plants.

---

[17] As suggested by Aristoteles (Meteorology book II-chapter 3rd): when water is heated in a vase, its vapor condenses, especially on the lid of the vase. He notes: "Experience has taught us that seawater reduced to steam becomes drinkable and the vaporized product, once condensed, does not replicate seawater ... wine and liquids, once vaporized, become water."

In both the cases a new, unknown element was discovered, something difficult to determine, but easy to find using the taste, alcohol.

Water added to seeds or fruits owing a high percentage of water[18], left some days in a container, could produce a nice palatable liquid from the pomace. We have news about beer[19], grapes and pomegranate wine, and hydromel obtained through the fermentation of honey, but certainly many similar beverages were tested and produced for centuries even if the history (especially from Egypt) reports only the most famous[20] (Fig. 22).

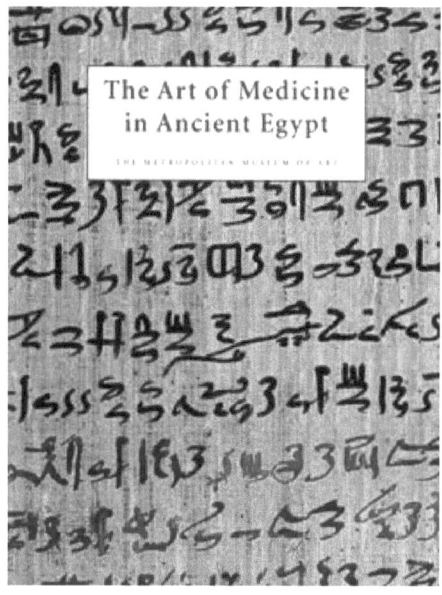

Fig. 22: James P. Allen & David T. Mininberg 2005: volume for the Exhibition at The Metropolitan Museum of Art, New York.

---

[18] Wilson C. Anne 2006: *A history of Wine distilling and spirits 500 BC – AD 2000*, Trowbridge, Wiltshire.

[19] Forbes, SAT HI (1965) 65-70; J. P. Arnold, Origin and History of Beer and Brewing (Chicago 1911) 41-184. L. F. Hartmann and A. L. Oppenheim, "On Beer and Brewing Techniques in Ancient Mesopotamia," J AOS Suppl. 10 (1950).

[20] James P.A. & D.T. Mininberg 2005: The Art of Medicine in Ancient Egypt. Exhibition at The Metropolitan Museum of Art, New York.

The percentage and possibility to increase the alcohol content, made the difference and brought the wine to important position, as a liquid which could be used to melt resins, purify animal fat, or employed as vehiculant or aggregating in compositions preserving it from rot. Wine became soon the base for preparing pharmaceutical compounds, including organic and inorganic ingredient for many diseases as the most ancient text report. Sweet fruits, however, could produce alcoholic liquid after fermentation, but the taste was different, often undrinkable. Again, somebody probably tried to boil the mash to take out the smell of the maceration, perhaps covering the pot with a dish positioned upside down and found that an interesting liquid was dropping down from the lid.

He discovered that the taste of maceration was disappearing and the liquid had something a special nice intoxicant taste. Surprisingly, he found that the liquid of the condensate was completely different from the ingredients boiling in the pot, even if it was coming from them. Gradually he changed the shape of the pots to collect better the liquid, learning that a specific process began automatically when the liquid in the pot started to vaporize raising the lid and forming condensation. So, he started to experiment with different compositions and ingredients to understand better the phenomenon and evaluate the properties of the liquids obtained.

But many years passed before he understood why the substance does not vaporize to the same temperature, and which was the real transformation of the whole. We do not know which ingredient or material was tested at the beginning, in turn thinking about that, we can find traces of the long path which brought the prehistoric people to find how distillation was discovered throughout the observation and the use of the cooking pots in different part of the world, far enough from each other to suggest that it was a casual personal achievement.

IV. Simple Apparatuses

One of the most interesting aspects in the history of the production of perfumes, galenic components and spirits is the invention and use of instruments, containers and vases, whose forms are forerunners of the alchemy instruments of glass and metal which during the centuries took the most bizarre shapes according to the eventual needs of the laboratory researches.

These objects are part of an essential supply of antique/modern labs and the ratio of acknowledgment for the Bronze Age. The evidence coming from different countries largely proves distillation does not need complicate apparatus to be made. Two simple pots joined by reeds of different dimensions, lids of clay, or other waterproof material to fix the pieces can perfectly work.

As largely demonstrated by Ana G. Valenzuela-Zapata, P. D. Buell, M. de la Paz Solano-Pérez, and H. Park with their paper on *"Huichol" Stills: A Century of Anthropology – Technology Transfer and Innovation"*, on East Asian stills and Mexican distillation, many solutions employing any kind of wood, reeds, clay, and metal specimens which may be found in different countries and cultures, all addressed in the production of alcohol, from seeds, roots, vegetables, fruits, honey, and milk (Fig. 23).

This evidence suggests that distillation has been and is mainly used to make alcoholic beverages, starting at a very early time.

Fig.23: Distillation of palm wine to give arrack from Amboina, The Moluccas, Indonesia (https://commons.wikimedia.org/wiki/File:Distillation_of_palm-wine,_Indonesia_Wellcome_M0005336.jpg).

This consideration is probably correct for many countries, except the circum-Mediterranean area where the knowledge of distillation seems equally employed in making alcoholic beverages, scented hydrosol, essential oils and pharmaceutical compounds for personal use and religion since the beginning. The difference mainly consists in assembling a correct apparatus, as alcohol distillation requires a simple device and low temperature, while perfume and medicines require an instrumental outfit composed of many elements (pots, strainers, funnels, bowls, spouted pots, lids etc.), often set together without a precise rule adapting household utensils to the purpose.

It is difficult to refuse the hypothesis that many simple and spouted pots of prehistoric cultures, could have been employed for distillation if we accept that today many people, in different parts of the world, are using the same pots and pieces of any kind of material as lids and spouts, to arrange apparatuses that have nothing in common with the shape of the standard distiller of glass and copper we well know. Here we have same examples from two distant part of the world.

The distillation *of* Arak at Bali (Fig. 24) is arranged around a central furnace under an earth container with a wood lid, and the liquor runs inside bamboo canes connecting with three clay pot receivers. The whole has nothing in common with the alchemical illustrations.

Fig. 24: Bali, distillation of Arak.

In Mexico at Oaxaca (Tierra Madre) the Mezcal (a kind of Tequila) is produced *en olla de barro* (in clay jars) in column distillation (Fig. 25) arranged on a close furnace heating the first pot that holds the second pot with a perforated base. Meanwhile, a large pumpkin spoon (connected with a reed passing through the pot wall) suspended in the middle collects the liquid dropping from the bottom of the cool, consisting in a metal concave basin receiving fresh water continuously (Fig. 26).

Fig. 25: Column system *en olla de barro* to still Mezcal.

Fig. 26: Station for distillation of Mezcal, Oaxaca Tierra Madre, Mexico.

The last evidence from Mexico, which seems the most improbable, is with the employment of a wood apparatus. The region where it survives is the ancient Tarascan Sub province in the Neo volcanic Axis of west-central Mexico, today inhabited by mix populations of Tarascan-Mexican and Hispano-Mexican that for centuries have carried out distillation in barrels[21]. Bourke in 1893 (68-69) describes the device, publishing a drawing of the assemble (Fig.27):

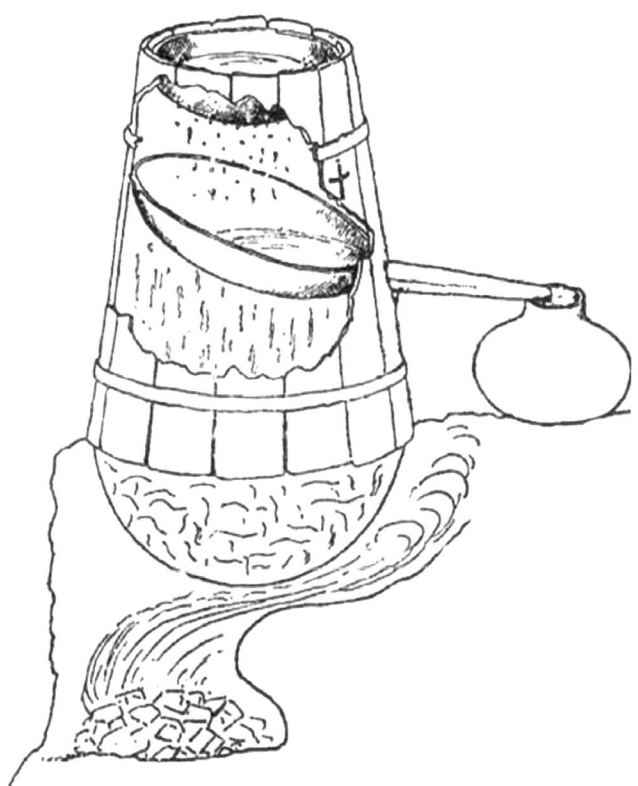

Fig. 27: Tarascan still apparatus, by Bourke 1893, 68.

---

[21] Bourke, J. G. (1893), Primitive Distillation among the Tarascoes. American Anthropologist, a. 6: 65–70.

"The still was erected at the edge of a vertical bank of hard clay, a situation which simplified labour very much. The whole apparatus was the most primitive kind, but the product was exceptionally good and clear.

*At **a** was the fire, with outlet for smoke at **b**; **c** and **d** were hoops, against which were placed the staves, secured on the outside by other hoops or circles apparently of willow. At **e** was the mashed mescal in a large earthen bowl; **f**, on top of the still, was another large bowl full of cold water, which was ladled out by an attendant as it became heated and supplied afresh.*

*The steam arising from the heated mescal condensed against the bottom of the bowl (**f**) filled with cold water and then dropped into a bowl (**g**) placed at angle. This bowl was called the cuchara or spoon From the cuchara the mescal ran out through the tube **k**, made of mescal stalk, into the olla or water jar **l**"***. The wooden barrel was very rude in construction, the gaping seams being closed with wet clay and gum***. I am far from committing myself to the proposition that the Mexican Indians were acquainted with distillation before the time of the conquest. Indeed, when and where distillation was first practised will perhaps never be known".*

I wonder who, on finding after twenty centuries, the remains of these distillation stations consisting in carbons and scattered fragments of earth, and clay, will recognise they were still apparatuses?

If we move in a Tunis household where a lady is making Neroli or Rose water (hydrosol), the subject changes from an alcoholic beverage to hydrosol, but with no freedom to assemble a distillatory apparatus with the objects available at home.

In this case the lady has arranged a curious apparatus made by a metal bucket on clay bricks, with a breast shaped clay top (the cool) holding a large metal tube passing through a ceramic flowerpot, positioned on bricks and cartoons, dropping the liquid inside a glass fiasco with the base of plastic (Fig. 28).

Fig. 28: Domestic distillation of Rose water at Tunis.

Then, finding after twenty centuries the remains of this dismantled apparatus, perhaps we could have the suspicion that it was a distiller, because the copper bucket, the pots with side holes, the metal pipe, and the glass bottle survive (plastic will not survive and the bricks are the same of the ruined house).

The examples we illustrated are not isolated, there are uncountable evidence from every country of people (including the nomads) employing simple objects and material that have nothing to do with the standard clay, copper and glass apparatuses and alembics to distil. Observing their abrupt solutions, we realize that many pots in use as early as the late Neolithic period could have been employed for the same purpose.

In the prehistory of distillation people could assemble apparatus using the same ploys employing earth, clay pots, barks, reeds, and leather, joining the pieces with mud and resin, arranging a furnace under a column of vases, or using a simple perforated cooking pot to produce alcoholic beverages, hydrosol, essential oils and more, without any "approved" alembic. What was important was the knowledge, not the use of specific objects that have been invented after many experiments to facilitate a well-known operation.

Regarding the question about what was distilled at the beginning, we should look at the containers for storing liquids to find if the production was addressed towards scented waters, essential oils, or alcoholic beverages, whose shape is quite different according the liquid preserved.

Most of them have been found in funerary context[22], in very good conditions, but those coming from the archaeological sites are fragmentary, and sometimes only the framework gives us the opportunity to speculate about the use and age.

However, dividing the archaeological material, mostly ceramics, in equipment for producing and in containers for storing, we face two distinct classes of objects that should have a direct relationship to each other, when they belong to the same culture.

So before analysing the possible ceramic shapes that were used to assemble the first distilling apparatuses, let us ask if in the same context there are suitable containers to keep the products of distillation, bearing in mind that, at the beginning, the distillation of organic substances produced liquids containing to varying degrees alcohol and essential oils that have been recognised after some time. It is therefore evident that at the first perfumed waters obtained by distillation, were very like the "waters" that are still produced today in a family context and in non-specialized rural environments (Fig. 29).

Besides, considering that wine production dates to the 5th millennium BC and from the worst wine (not just grape) you can always get a good brandy,

---

[22] Even if, the presence of these containers in the tombs is not a confirmation of production, but of trade and use of them.

it is very likely that boiling wine to improve its taste brought to the discovery of distillation. While herbs and flowers boiled to keep the therapeutic compound and scent entered the scenario in a second moment.

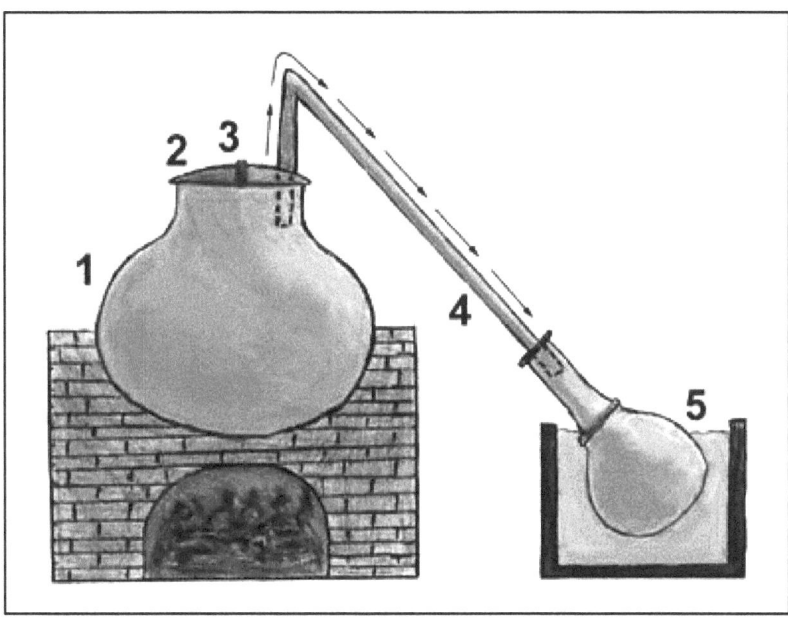

Fig. 29: Pattern of Attar distillation, with clay pots and reeds Bhapka, India

However, for alcoholic beverage, we find the same jars used for wine and beer, and we can only watch with suspicion askoi, rythons and multi-decorated clay horns, produced all around the Mediterranean, to speculate they were made for special alcoholic drinks.

For essential oils, hydrosol and medical products, the situation is different, as the substances are more delicate and require different precautions for their use and conservation.

♍

Valeriana officinalis L.

V. The Strainer

A separate discussion lies with the strainer, which is an important component for proper distillation of liquor and aromatic waters.

The strainer was probably the first component added for the distilling of organic materials. In fact, its use as a separator between two pots, or container of the material, allows a better production of a clear liquid.

The strainer is one of the most common household utensils used mainly for the cleaning of grains, the production of beer and cheese, and steam cooking.

Fig. 30: Simple bamboo strainer.

It is a simple device that you can make by strapping straw, bamboo, perforating barks, dried pumpkins, hardened skin, or wood (Fig. 30).

The first examples of terracotta appear almost together with the first ceramics in different parts of the world. But the folk testimony of the continued use of the strainer made of organic material in many rural and primitive environments suggests that most of the strainers were perishable and that only those used for an important and prestigious employ were made of clay or metal. In the still apparatuses circulating today, including the primitive-rural specimens we find three different kinds of strainers, the same ones used in antiquity.

- The detached strainer.

The detached strainer is a component of different types ranging from the simple flat plate (Fig.31) to the funnel turned inside (inverted strainer funnel). Of course, the size is variable, suitable for the vessel on which it leans. The first appears at the end of the Neolithic period in the circum-Mediterranean area. Some specimens about 7,000 years old, from Poland, recently analysed were probably employed to make cheese[23].

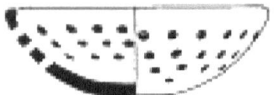

Fig. 31: Strainer bowl 5000 BC Tell Brak.

The second seems to have Slovakia origins[24] dating back to the 3rd - 4th millennium BC. The shape arrived in Anatolia around the 2nd mill. BC.

Fig. 32: Cylindrical strainer with inverted funnel inside in a modern column device.

---

[23] Mélanie Salque, Peter I. Bogucki, Joanna Pyzel, Iwona Sobkowiak-Tabaka, Ryszard Grygiel, Marzena Szmyt & Richard P. Evershed 2013: Earliest evidence for cheese making in the sixth millennium BC in northern Europe in Nature 493, 522–525 (24 January 2013).
[24] Nemejcová-Pavúková, V. 1979: Nálezy bolerázskej skupiny z Vrbového. Archeol. rozhl., 31, s. 393.

But the type, still today, is largely employed as an additional element in copper column devices (Fig. 32).

-Strainer flask.

It consists of a high cylindrical flask with completely drilled walls to be inserted inside a jar. The most ancient is a large specimen coming from Macedonia Dikili Tash (Fig. 33), dating back to the Late Neolithic II (around 7000 BC). It is a well-known item interpreted as a Cheese - strainer, in which recent analyses found only remains of bee wax.

The evidence suggests the object was a beehive or a sort of filter involved in the production of hydromel. The site returned also substantial evidence of consumption of grapes supposing employed in making wine.

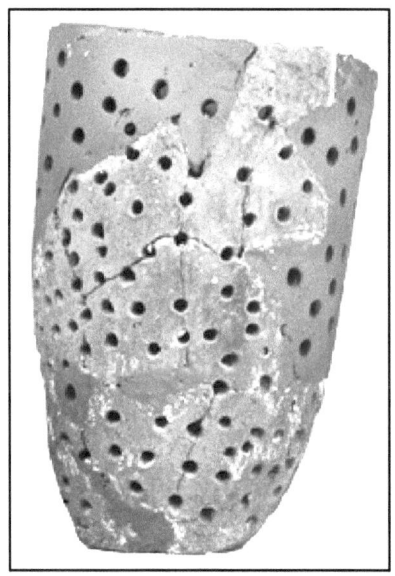

Fig. 33: Strainer flask from Dikili Tash Macedonia, Salonicco Museum.

At the end of the Ubaid period in Mesopotamia (4000-3800 BC), we find at Tepe Gawra a large specimen of strainer flask (bottle)[25] in the same context from which the channel pots with holes through the inside come.

---

[25] Arthur J. Tobler Excavations at Tepe Gawra, vol. II, Philadelphia 1950, 239, n. 360. Strainer, light buff ware; h. 33,6, d. 22,2. G5-1339. XI-A, 6G.

After centuries, we find the strainer flask, more similar to the specimen from Macedonia, in Indus valley where around 3000 BC the type seems to have had a large diffusion (Fig. 34). Many specimens of different size (between ten to 35 cm high) have been found at Harappa, Mohengio Daro, and Dvarak (the lost city), conserved in the National Museum of New Delhi (Harappa gallery). Given the difference in the size of pots and holes, the possibility of being bee hives seems far away.

Fig. 34: Strainer flasks from Mohengio Daro, Dwaraka and Harappa New Dheli Museum.

- Strainer jar.

Needham considers the jar with the perforated base is the main element of the traditional Chinese steam-cooking, from which the China's distillation apparatus was born (see below chapter VIII). However, the method was widely known in the Aegean at the beginning of the 2nd millennium BC (chapter XI), and today is normally employed in Mexico to make Mezcal (Fig. 25); in Morocco copper column devices for hydrosol; in India for *attars* and of course in China.

VI. Storing pots: a case of comparison between Cyprus and Egypt.

For fragrant ointments and perfumed waters (hydrosol), we find some typological distinction for the dissimilar consistence of the liquid (oil and water), which requires a vase with a different mouth and rim.

-The ointments made melting essential oils with vehiculant oil (Olive, Moringa, Balanites Aegyptiaca, Almond) are better preserved in bottles with a narrow neck, small mouth opening, and mushroom disk rim, which help in distributing directly on the skin the ointment and in recovering the last drop of the precious liquid.

It seems that Egypt invented the shape during the third millennium BC[26], first in clay and then carving the bottle in alabaster, implemented for millennia all around the Mediterranean in thousands of clay, stone, glass, and metal versions (Fig. 35). There is no doubt that the solution to keep the fragrant oils in stone containers, better preserved away from the light and heat the fattish liquid was optimal, even though it is likely that the cylindrical shape of later specimens has been influenced by the first containers of reed used to keep kohl for eyes and other cosmetics.

---

[26] Ritual vessel (hes-jar) Egyptian, Early Dynastic Period to Old Kingdom, Dynasty 1–, 2960–2465 B.C. From Abydos, Osiris-Khentyamentyu Temple, area 215. 1903: excavated by William Matthew Flinders Petrie for the Egypt Exploration Fund, assigned to the Egypt Exploration Fund in the division of finds by the government of Egypt (Fig. 29,1).

Fig. 35: 1, Ritual vessel (hes-jar) Egyptian, Early Dynastic Period 2960–2465 B.C. Museum of Fine Arts Boston; 2, Alabastron 3 4 dynasty Metropolitan Museum NY; 3; Egyptian Alabastron, Limassol district Museum, Cyprus

The shape has been the most used for storing and trading oil perfumes from the X century BC until the Medieval time. In the same period, we find many coroplastic perfume bottles (askoi), representing animals, objects, and people with the same disk rim (Fig. 36).

Fig. 36: Monkey shaped perfume bottle V cent. BC Iraklion Museum, Crete.

It is a kind of distinguishing element that still characterize glass bottles for oil perfumes coming from Egypt and Near East.

According to the archaeological evidence the first civilisation which, after Egypt adopted the shape, was the Cypriot, around the turn of the second millennium BC. The specimens in Red Polished have been found both in the funeral and domestic contexts suggesting the oil perfumes were commonly used in daily life and as traditional grave goods (Fig.37).

The type characterized by the rounded body persists throughout the Bronze Age and the Geometric period, becoming the best witness of the demand for the perfumes of Cyprus and its trade all around the Mediterranean, before becoming the typical Greek Aryballos.

Fig. 37: Perfumes bottles from Pyrgos/Mavroraki perfumery, Cyprus 2000-1900 BC.

Besides, the Cypriot Early Bronze age repertoire includes a small pear-shaped flash with a straight neck/mouth and cut away rim, which has a parallel evolution in small jugs with a straight tubular neck/mouth and small juglets with cutaway mouth on small cylindrical neck (Fig. 38 a, b).

Fig. 38: a, Early Bronze age pear shaped Flash, Copenhagen National Museum; b Early Bronze age tubular neck bottle with a ring on top, Met. Museum New York; c, Orthodox silver sprinkler from Cyprus, private collection, Cyprus.

Its proper use is to sprinkle hydrosol like the well-known rosewater sprinklers (*aspergillum*) widely used today in Orthodox (Fig.38 c), Arab, Persian, Indian and Jewish traditions, for religious occasions and welcoming guests.

Fig. 39: a-b, Cyprus Middle Bronze age White Painted aspergillum with the side opening to host the thumb during the sprinkling, and c, Cypriot Byzantine version of glass around VI A.D; all conserved in the Metropolitan Museum New York.

The Middle Bronze age Cypriot flash with the straight neck furnished on the side and an oval opening near a short vertical handle, seems a direct evolution of the Early Bronze age type, comfortably foldable overlapping the thumb over the oval opening to spray the liquid more easily (Fig. 39).

This flash/juglet sprinkler or *aspergillum* realised in many different styles and materials remained virtually unchanged over the centuries, adopted by different cultures, religions, and people that from immemorial time produce once a year in domestic environment hydrosol of rose, orange or other flowers for the same purpose.

Of course, the contemporary presence of both the shapes in Cyprus suggests that the island has started to produce essential oils and hydrosols in the Early Bronze age, probably learning the technology from other countries.

A quantitative comparison of such objects in the funerary outfits of nearby civilizations, calculated in percentage of graves, takes us back to the Pharaonic environment; where many Cypriot perfume bottles have been found, together with pots and glasses of the local repertoire.

The difference between the second millennium BC Egypt and Cyprus production is in the addressing and use of these fragrances. For rich people in Egypt and for everybody in Cyprus, where no social distinction existed, while the production of hydrosol and oil perfumes was still a traditional activity, performed in a family and community location[27].

---

[27] A worthy *excursus* on the most antique perfume containers of the Cyprus Bronze Age is found in the book of Desmond Morris on the art of ancient Cyprus, where the scholar attempts to reconsider the edited pottery typology of the Swedish Cyprus expedition published in 1962; D. Morris 1985. *The Art of Ancient Cyprus,* Oxford Phaidon.
P. Dikaios & J.R. Stewart 1962. *The Swedish Cyprus Expedition* vol. IV, part 1A, Lund.

Coriandrum sativum L.

VII. The alembic head.

Due to its peculiar shape, the alembic head is the only part of an apparatus which is possible to be recognisable when it is detached.

Its creation does not witness the knowledge or ignorance of distillation, as the technology born before the alembic and it was the distillation which created the alembic not the contrary.

Assuming that, before the appearance of glass and copper it was possible to arrange an apparatus using artefacts of clay, mud, wood, reed, leather, straw, and bone, normally available in a domestic or rural environment, it is my intention to underline that the *alembic*, like any other *instrumental pot*, has evolved from the simple to the more elaborate and functional form over a long period, keeping the shape from common spouted jars, jugs, and cooking pots with rounded base.

It is very likely that the people probably modified the form to improve its functionality, after oral suggestions of merchants and walking healers, who described technology and equipment seen in other contexts.

In historical terms, the word alembic, whose origin is sufficiently debated[28], appears in the "European and Arab" vocabulary after the 1200 when the *glass spouted onion head* from the Middle East to Europe was extensively known and employed. However, due the fragility of the

---

[28] Dioscurides (Materia Medica 70 A.D.) mentions the *ambix* for sublimation, referring to a vase with a small opening, while in 1200 A.D. Ibn al-Awwam in his *Kitab al-Filaha* (*Book of Agriculture*), describes the *anbik* giving the recipe for rosewater.

material and the possibility of re-melting the glass, few specimens survived before the 15th century.

The most ancient seem to be an Egyptian example of the XI century conserved in the Getty Museum at Malibu (Los Angeles), which is an important element of comparison with Nubian prototypes of 2000 BC; this will be discussed later. Concerning glass versions, whose appearance should coincide with the invention of distillation, it is useful to remember that the first report is that testified by Zosimos of Panopolis (4th cent. AD) describing the Maria the Jewish apparatuses (Dibikos and Tribikos) made of glass and copper (Fig. 11).

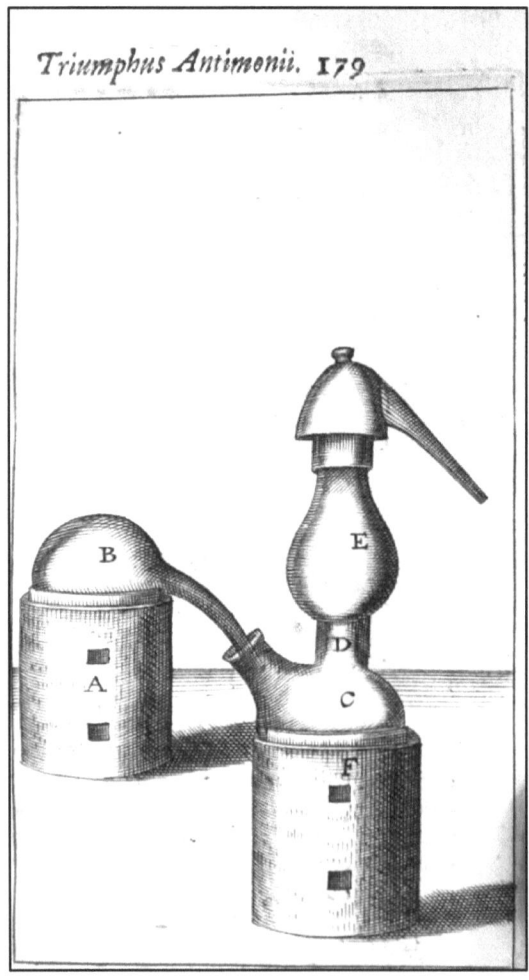

Fig. 40: Theodor Kerckring, 1671, *Commentarius in currum triumphalem Antimonii Basilii Valentini* (Amsterdam), p. 179.

The maximum diameter of specimens found is 24 centimetres, but most are about 15cm. Regarding its engagement, the alchemical illustrations and the results of analyses made on the content of some specimens[29], testify that they were almost exclusively employed for chemical and metalloids extractions (Fig. 40)[30].

Fig. 41: Traditional clay alembic XIX cent. Cyprus Ethnographic Museum Yeroskypos

Their use in preparing medical compounds and potions is confirmed by the illustrations of the alchemical books and vintage paintings, often allegoric. Given the small size, fragility, and poor handling, they were not used for producing alcoholic beverages, for which copper alembics soon appeared to be more appropriate, and without limits of dimensions,

---

[29] S. Moorhouse 1972: Medieval Distilling-Apparatus of Glass and Pottery (Fig. 25; 88-89) referring fragments of distilling apparatuses dating around the half of the XV century.
[30] The recent discovery of an alchemist' laboratory at Wittenberg, confirms the glass alembics used mainly for Antimuonium, Arsenic and Nitric acid.: Curry A. The Alchemist's Tale. Archaeology, magazine, Jan/Feb 2016, Vol. 69 Issue 1, 36.

although terracotta devices remained the most economical solution up to a recent past (Fig. 41), especially in Cyprus and Greek islands. Though the glass alembics were available, they were never practically used to produce spirits and perfumes, which needed much larger pots.

The production of glass alembic was also limited to the presence and skill of the glass masters, who could blow and shape the object.

We must remember that glass blowing was discovered in the first century BC on the Siro-Judean coast and that the alembic head was certainly not among the first objects made. Though the proximity to Alexandria, home of Mary the Jewish and the most ancient descriptions of alembics, suggests that the first specimens were made in that geographic area, probably copying clay patterns, normally employed, and circulating. The description of the Dibikos and Tribikos of Maria the Hebrew reported by Zosimos mentions the employment of glass and copper tubes (Fig. 42).

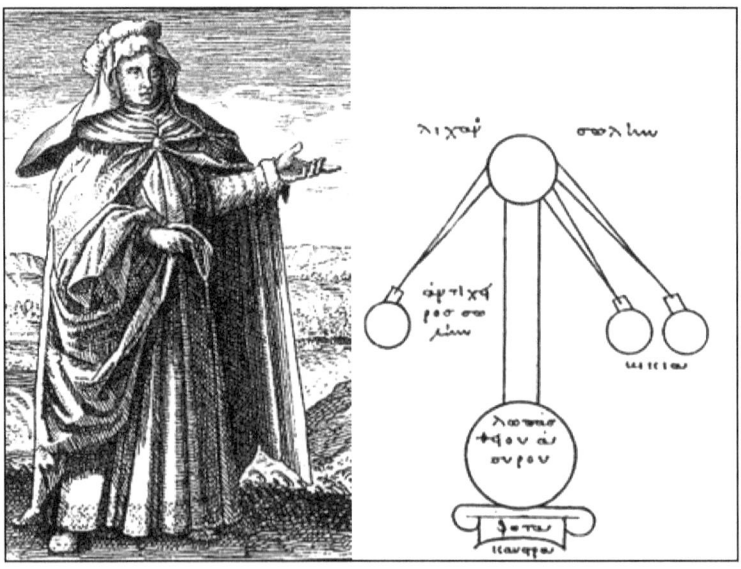

Fig. 42: Mary the Jewess and *her Tribikos*

After the 3rd century AD, still in the Egyptian entourage, despite the exception of a late drawing, nothing survived of such smart and complicate inventions that mark the steps of our knowledge. They utilized three or four diverse still sorts incorporating one with three bronze tubes[31].

Their objective was not to distil spirits but rather to get substances, for example, sulphur, mercury, antimony, and arsenic, keeping in mind the end goal to adjust the outer synthesis of base metals and shading them gold. This was a piece of a custom practice, "a recuperating and discharge for all torment from the spirit." (*Phusika kai mustika*, 200 BC). During the time spent delivering "fire" from base metal, it was thought, the chemist's spirit would thusly turn out to be progressively "red hot," or nearer to paradise.

It turns out that the first devices of glass had copper tubes as spouts that copy clay apparatuses for chemical distillation. These were probably already used as clay extension pipes (such as Taxila and Shakan Dheri) or copper, as a distillation of acids and metalloids was not possible with marsh reeds which could not withstand the developed temperatures.

It seems clear that at the time the knowledge of distillation had been acquired for a long time, so much so that it was used not only for alcoholic beverages and perfumes, but for truly scientific experiments.

Besides, the dome alembic appears as the result of a long evolution that reached the optimum after the third century A.D., before becoming part of an exclusive environment such as that of alchemy, from which the modern chemical laboratories, which still use the same devices, come in direct sequence.

---

[31] Taylor, F. Sherwood 1937. The Visions of Zosimos, *AX*, x, 88; *Symbols in Greek Alchemical Writings*, *AAX*, 64; Taylor, F. Sherwood 1950: Alchemists, Founders of Modern Chemistry. pp. 38–39, New York.

In view of the importance of this object in the history of distillation, we will try to make the reverse path of its evolution, looking for the modifications supported by the pattern. To make this, I will analyse the four elements that compose the alembic head: Dome, Spout, Channel, and Neck.

- **The Dome.**

This component has the function of the expansion tank or vessel, hosting the vapour that after saturating the close and cooler space condenses. Inverting the alembic pot, the Dome corresponds to the rounded bottom (upside down) of pots without base support, which belong to a specific typology or cultural preference. Vases with a round base, i.e. without a flat, ring or hinted base that ensure the static of the vessel, are rare in the Neolithic period, while they become common in many circum-Mediterranean cultures since the beginning of the Early Bronze Age around the 3000 BC (Fig. 43).

Fig. 43: Predynastic Naqada Cooking pot, in the antiquarian market.

The transformation mainly regarded cooking pots, determining the adoption of different potting practices, including the use of moulds (or shaped pits) to make a globular body or round-based bodies.

In the next chapter on Mesopotamia, I will mention some specimens which have the same body and a complete different neck/rim, probably made using a sort of mould. At the end of the 4th / beginning 3rd millennium BC, we find the first vessels with round base mainly in Egypt, Mesopotamia, and Palestine, few in Anatolia and Aegean, together with many pots with a just hinted base.

Around the beginning of the II millennium BC there was a pottery revolution in the Mediterranean, mainly in Cyprus, where the round base almost completely replaced the flat in most ceramic typologies.

-The Spout.

The Spout in terms of distillation is the pipe which carries the condensate to be collected in a pot receiver.

Considering the possible variable distance between the still and collector, reeds or bamboo canes are currently employed in many rural factories engaged in producing alcoholic beverages and perfumes, following ancient traditional systems. The reeds have some benefits, first because they cost nothing, second, they do not keep the heat (working as refreshing tubes), thirdly they do not need maintenance or to be cleaned, but only substituted. However, the inset requires adequate openings in the pot, to seal the connection with lute, fixed strips, and to prevent vapour dispersion, as we can see in some photos (Fig. 24, 25, 26 and 29) regarding the making of Mezcal in Mexico or Attar in India. It follows that to work as an alembic, a pot should have a rounded body and a spouted opening on the side, two components that we find at the end of the 4th millennium BC in different categories of vases, including jugs, amphoras and jars.

However, beside the standard categories, another spouted pot with rounded body, not belonging to the above classes appears at the beginning of the 3rd millennium BC. The difficult attribution to a specific category of pitchers, amphoras or jars suggested to the archaeologists of the last century to give it the definition of the *teapot* (Fig. 44).

Fig. 44: Tea pot Hebron, Israel 3000 BC.

A name of fantasy that created some confusion in the interpretation of these vessels, especially in a non-academic environment. In this type of vessel, it is interesting to note that the position of the spout under the neck attachment it is like the glass item ones (Fig. 45).

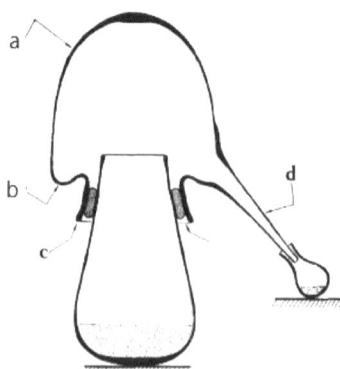

Fig. 45: Standard glass alembic by C.C. Moore, in S. Moorhouse 1972.

This shape evolved mainly in the Levant, Near East and Cyprus, while in the Indo-Pakistan region the spouted pot, later employed in the distillation, took the shape of a low rounded large spouted bowl (Fig. 46).

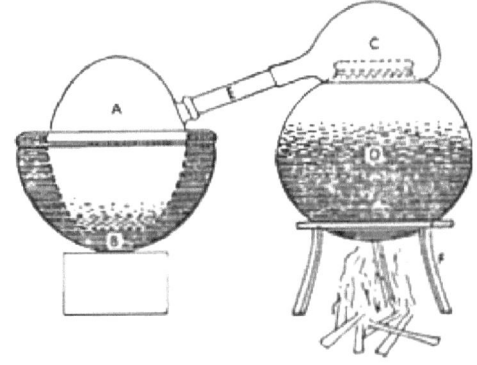

Fig. 46: Original drawings by Marshall.

Still reconstructed from finds at Taxila, Punjab (after Marshall, 1951). apparatus dates from 1st century B.C.-A.D.

In the same regions (Pakistan, the Indus valley and India) we find clay tubes that connect the spout of head and receiver mouth, dating back from the 1st BC (Fig. 47) to the 4th century AD (Fig. 48). They are (occasional) accessories, intentionally enriched with circular ribs in relief and discoid fastener at the extremity to better join with the alembic head spout[32].

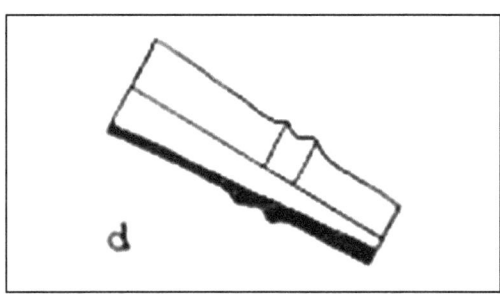

Fig. 47: Terracotta tube from Shaikhan Dherì: by Dani 1966: fig. 34.3.

---

[32] Allchin F.R., 1979b, 774, observes that "the terracotta tube has two appliqued bands around centre, giving it the likeness of a piece of bamboo". Reported first by Dani 1966: fig.34.3.

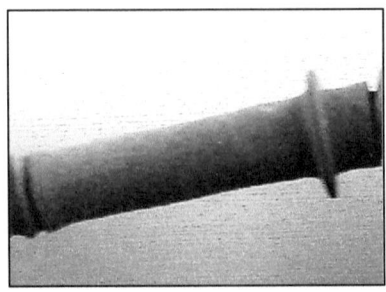

Fig. 48: Terracotta tube of Taxila apparatus.

Until here we have two elements joined in the same pot, and we suppose that the evolution continued with the adding of the other two, the channel and the everted neck/rim in the same entourages, but things did not go that way.

The channel.

It is the component positioned between the neck and the spout, having the function to collect the liquid of condensation by conveying it into the spout. It is a proper component of the glass alembics which we do not find in the rural apparatus to still alcoholics and perfumes, though it has a long life back in the history of distillation. According to the archaeological evidence this component first appears in Mesopotamia at the end of the 4th and very beginning of the 3rd millennium BC (details in the chapter), disappearing after 400 years. Its function is enough debated, but the position around the mouth of the pot is a technological ploy that has been employed for many different cases (see p.75). After more than 1000 years, around the 2000 BC Hittites took the suggestion, making a pot with a channel inside (see p.90), shaped like a teapot to distil ceremonial liquids.

The idea spread to the Mediterranean and was reused for various types of ceramics related to distillation until the end of the second millennium BC (see p. 94-98). After the beginning of the first millennium, the hidden channel inside the vase became an element of prestige and value for cult vases (kernoi) and luxury vessels for drinking alcoholic beverages, entering the technological repertoire of ceramic workshops.

The neck.

The straight and flared neck is an important component of the alembic head, as it favours the perfect closure with the ampulla or "cucurbita" avoiding dispersion of vapour. In the clay alembic it is less common, and in some it is completely absent. The truncated-conical flared shape undoubtedly recalls the vases of the Bell-Beaker Culture, 2900 - 1800 BC, which spreads through the prehistoric Western Europe from the Late Neolithic until the Early Bronze Age, arriving in the West Mediterranean islands. However, the same form of neck had been already present in the 6000 BC Halaf culture in Upper Mesopotamia (Fig. 49), Zagros Massif and along the southern slopes of Ararat, leaving an indelible imprint in the Ubaid Mesopotamian culture of the beginning of the 4th millennium BC (see chapter IX).

Fig. 49: Tell Halaf jar, Aleppo archaeological Museum.

Though, the first time we find a conical truncated base, which could have suggested the flange element of the alembic head is in Minoan culture of 2000 BC, that produced a strainer tureen pattern (which is the subject of the chapter XI), which was probably involved in domestic and palace production of scented water or alcoholic beverage until the end of the Aegean Bronze age.

The same suggestion probably reached the Nubian kingdom of Kerma, later conquered by Egypt, that produced in the second millennium BC a pot which is almost the exact copy of the standard alembic head (chapter XII), including the flange and shape, length, and position of the spout. Besides, the presence of these vessels in Nubia greatly justifies the spread of the type in Cyprus at the beginning of the 2nd millennium BC, as the Nubian and Cypriot ceramic wares of 1800-1700 BC are exceptionally similar, not only for the colour and type of vessels, but the incised decoration filled with white pasta to highlight the design (Fig. 50 and 51).

Fig. 50: Black Pol. Bowl and Flask, Cyprus Early/Middle Bronze age, antiquary market.

Fig. 51: Black Pol. Bowl Kerma Classic group, Middle Bronze age, Christie's Hong Kong.

VIII. China

In 2011 in the region of Nanchang, capital of East China's Jiangxi was discovered the Liu He (92-59 BC) tomb, grandson of Emperor Wu, the greatest ruler of the Han Dynasty (206 BC-AD 24). Liu was given the title "Haihunhou" (Marquis of Haihun[33]) after he was deposed as emperor after only 27 days, dethroned by the royal clan because of his lack of talent and morals[34]. The excavation of the tomb, now considered one of the richest found in China ended in 2016 after a careful and meticulous work to recover and restore the ten thousand objects that made up the outfit.

Among the innumerable precious gold, jade and bronze handicrafts, the attention of archaeologists has focused on the well-preserved copper distiller of large dimensions, which takes the oldest evidence of Chinese alcohol distillation back 1000 years.

The specimen consisting in a cylinder open on the base with a straight cylindrical neck in the middle, it has a grid on the top, two opposite spouts on the shoulder and three rings on the lower body for handling (Fig. 52).

There is no additional news about the other parts of the apparatus that we suppose was a column, composed of clay or copper elements. Of course, the first consideration is on the evolved form of the object that attests a long knowledge of the distillation technique.

---

[33] "Haihunhou" = Marquis of Haihun, which is the ancient name of a very small kingdom in the north of Jiangxi.
[34] http://www.newhistorian.com/excavation-haihunhou-tomb-china-completed/7382/;
http://www.ecns.cn/visual/hd/2016/03-02/88168.shtml

Fig. 52: Copper distiller from the Liu He Tomb 59 AD, East China Nanchang[35].

This helps confirm the theory of John Needham, who in 1980 published the encyclopaedic treaty on the History of Science in China[36], affirming that the first distillation apparatus progressed from the traditional Chinese steaming pot used to cook food. Probably he was not far from the realty considering the age of the Herbarium written by "Red Emperor" Shen Nung. For Needham, the Chinese story starts at the end of the Neolithic period to which dates the first smart shape of cooking pot, which unified in one vase the elements of the fire tripod stand with the pot for boiling food. We are speaking about the *Lì* (or Ting), the Neolithic cooking pot whose body is provided of three vacuum conical feet in the middle of which you can arrange the fire[37] (Fig. 53).

---

[35] http://www.ecns.cn/visual/hd/2016/03-02/ 88168.shtml
[36] Needham 1980: Vol. V, Chemistry and Chemical Technology. Part IV: Spagyrical Discovery and Invention: Apparatus, Theories and Gifts.
[37] Andersson, J. G. 'Prehistoric sites in Honan.' BM FEA, 1947,19, I. Bulletin no. 19 of the Museum of Far Eastern Antiquities. H.R. Li The Chinese alcoholic culture Shanxi People's Publishing House, Taiyuan (1995) [In Chinese].

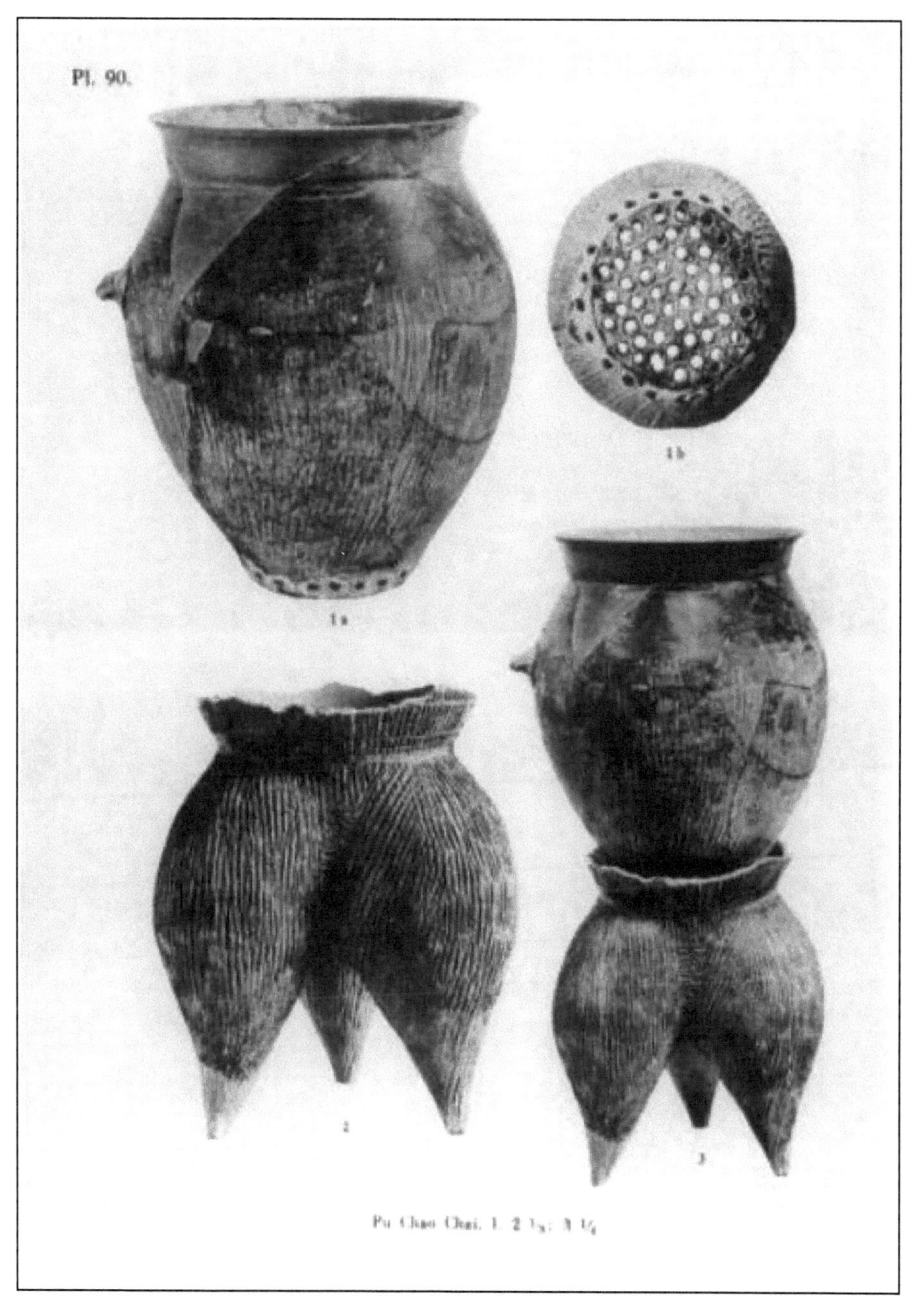

Fig.53: From J.G. Andersen 1947, Pl. 90: *(1a) Tsèng Steamer (1b) Perforated Bottom of Steamer; (2) Li Boiler with three hollowed legs; (3) Hsìen assembled from Tsèng and Lì..*

The shape survived into historic times, becoming the traditional *Tsèng*, a steamer formed by the tripod-pot and a strainer base jar. According to Needham, this peculiar vase had different degrees of evolution until it became a device to still (Fig.54):

1- *location of a second hole mouth pot, with the base completely perforated as a strainer, at the top of the first;*
2- *addition of a bowl lid on the top of the second pot;*
3- *the second pot is transformed in a hole base and mouth pot, and a movable filter is inserted between the two vases;*
4- *a bowl is positioned on the strainer inside the upper pot;*

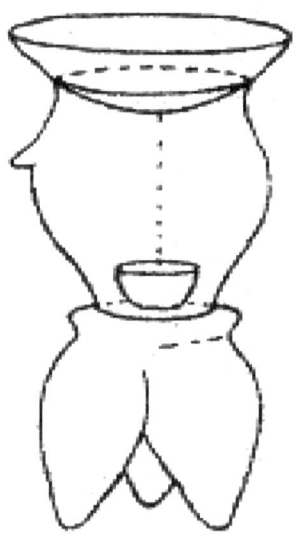

Fig.54: From Needham Fig. 1473[38].

5- *the bowl lid is shaped to help the dropping of the condense.*

---

[38] Needham J. 1980: *Fig. 1473C. "Conjectural design of the most ancient Mongolian~chinese still type. A bowl of cooling water caps the upper vessel (tslng) and a collecting-bowl stands upon its perforated bottom (or of course on the grating of a hsien when the two vessels were combined into one). The li below provides the vapours, and the distillate collects in the bowl, equipped subsequently with a side-tube".*

6- *In few words, the traditional Li evolved first in a steaming pot and then gradually in a device formed by 5 elements: 1) tripod pot 2) holed base and mouth pot 3) strainer 4) deep bowl 5) conical lid.*

In this path of evolution, we see that the key element which made the difference was the strainer and its strategic position as a filter and support of the collector. With his theory, Needham [39] confirms that the understanding of the distillation process came from the experience acquired in food-cooking, proving with in the case of China the first apparatus was a direct transformation of the steaming pot for food[40].

According to him the evolution of the knowledge probably runs side by side with the invention of new shapes of pot, and from the first examples arranged superimposing two standard pots, all the different solutions come. Of course, his opinion about the use of it goes to alcoholic beverages, the production of which the **Nanchang** distiller seems to refer to. However, the absence of any contemporary specimen of clay or metal makes it difficult to rethink the evolutionary and typological path followed by the Chinese craftsman who made that copper device, which surprisingly after more than 2000 years, has much in common with professional distillers sold around the world. Besides, the distiller found at **Nanchang** seems to look more like the Aegean/Minoan apparatuses of the 2000 BC (which I will discuss in chapter XI), than to any prototypes described and graphically illustrated by Needham[41].

---

[39] Needham J. 1980: *Science and Civilisation in China, vol. V, Chemistry and Chemical Technology. Part IV: Spagyrical Discovery and Invention: Apparatus, Theories and Gifts*. Cambridge Un. Press

[40] An earlier sketch of this by us has been reproduced in Thurm, H. G. 1978. Shao Chui, *Gebramuer Wein im alten China*. Team-Fachvedlli. Karlstein aI M Sonderausgabe der Alkohol-Industrie, Ed. p. 18.

[41] Ho Ping-Yü & Joseph Needham (1959) The Laboratory Equipment of the Early Mediæval Chinese Alchemists, Ambix, 7:2, 58-112, DOI: 10.1179/amb.1959.7.2.58.

It is interesting to note that the team of Patrick Mc Govern, specialized in archaeometry investigation on ancient alcoholic beverages, published in 2004[42] the results of a research made on the production of different kinds of wines and alcoholic beverages in China since the 7th millennium BC. In 2008 the results of similar investigation made on pots from Greece and Crete containing residues of fermented and alcoholic beverages[43] that do not seem very different from each other was also published.

The whole of data largely justifies in China 1st century BC the acquaintance of an advanced technology of distilling spirits, probably destined for the exclusive consumption of an elite belonging to the members of the imperial family and their court, which seems to have inherited from Greece a knowledge born in the Minoan/Aegean in 2000 BC. As a bronze specimen, the distiller of Liu He tomb, leaves no room for different interpretations, as it is often the case of ceramics whose employ is frequently misunderstand. The specimen is the central part of a column apparatus, the only part which cannot be misinterpret. It is very probable that the other parts of the device were next to it in the tomb and were not recognized, as their shape is not unlike that of the characteristic ceramic or bronze vessels of that time. However, other bronze specimens found in the tomb show details in the manufacture that suggest their

---

[42] Patrick E. McGovern, Juzhong Zhang, Jigen Tang, Zhiqing Zhang, Gretchen R. Hall, Robert A. Moreau, Alberto Nun~ ez, Eric D. Butrym, Michael P. Richards, Chen-shan Wang, Guangsheng Cheng, Zhijun Zhao, and Changsui Wang, 2004: Fermented beverages of pre- and proto-historic China, in PNAS, vol. 101 no. 51 Patrick E. McGovern, 17593–17598, doi: 10.1073/pnas.0407921102.

[43] Patrick E. McGovern, Donald L. Glusker, Lawrence J. Exner and Gretchen R. Hall, 2008: The Chemical Identification of Resinated Wine and a Mixed Fermented Beverage in Bronze-Age Pottery Vessels of Greece, in Archaeology Meets Science: Biomolecular Investigations in Bronze age Greece; The Primary Scientific Evidence, 1997-2003, ed. Y. Tzedakis et al-, 169-218. Oxford: Oxbow.

coming from the same workshop or being part of a set for special drinking including the apparatus to produce it.

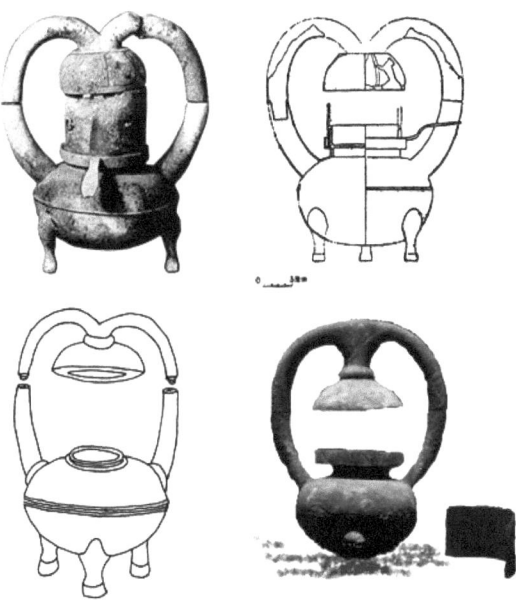

Fig.55: Han period sublimation device: a) the Rainbow vessel, b-c from Chhangsha Hunan, d) from the Liu He tomb.

In the same grave was also found a bronze specimen for sublimation, the same already found in other tombs of the Han period at Chhangsha, Hunan (1st century BC, 1st century A.D) used for the extraction of mercury[44]. The dimensions are closely similar for all (height about 34cm). The first specimen (a) reported by Needham as exhibited "during the second world war (in 1943) in the Institute of Cultural Studies of the University of Nanking (then located at Chhengtu, Szechuan) has an inscription self-naming the vessel: *Yen Ong Chu thung kung teng i chu,* i.e. "one *Rainbow Vessel* belonging *to Old Master Yen*" (Fig. 55). This type of distiller of

---

[44] Ping-Yù & Needham 1959, 84-87.
Another example is illustrated in the *Hsi Chhing Ku Chien170* (Catalogue of Ancient Mirrors and Bronzes of the Imperial Collection in the Library of Western Serenity) by Liang Shih-Cheng in 1751 (ch. 30, also Second Supplement, 1793, ch. 13, pp. *33b,34a).*

sublimation was named by Andreas Livanius (1540-1616) "Circulation apparatus with side tubes"[45]. The device is well known for the drawings of J. French (1651) and to have been used by Lavoisier in 1769[46] for its chemical experiments to transform water in the earth (Fig. 56).

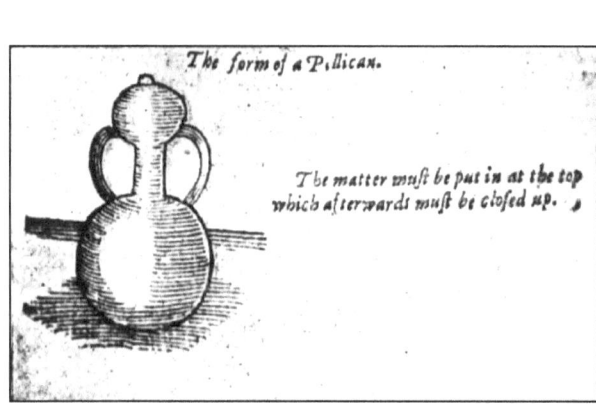

Fig. 56: Pelican flash. John French, The Art of Distillation (London 1651): and a version in glass still in production.

The version in glass is still in production, with a possible extension on top. As far as I know the most ancient example of this sublimator is the "Rainbow vessel" of the 1st century BC, mentioned by Needham, probably just invented by "The Old Master Yen"[47]. He was not only an artisan, but an erudite physician whose alchemical knowledge was not inferior to those of his colleagues living in the cultured Mediterranean environment, when the Roman Empire was at its utmost smartness.

---

[45] Alchemiae, Andreae Libavii Poet Physici Rotemburg, Francofurti, Iohannes Saurius, 1597.

[46] Lavoisier Antonie-Laurent, 1792: System der antiphologistischen Chemie. Aus dem Französischen übersetzt und mit Anmerkungen und Zusätzen versehen von D. Sigismund Friedrich Hermbstädt. 2 Bde in 1.8° Berlin

[47] About the figure of Old Master Yen, Birrell A. 1999: Chinese Mythology: An Introduction, J. Hopkins ed. JHU: 63-65.

IX. Mesopotamia: the cradle of civilizations.

Despite the many attempts to usurp the primacy, Mesopotamia and Egypt are still considered the greatest early civilizations of the western world.

Their evolution in the field of control of natural resources and high technical achievement runs parallel, passing through rough contemporary periods of prosperity and advanced knowledge, separated by periods of relative obscurity, when less civilized peoples overrun from nearby until about 530 BC, when both succumbed to the Persian invasion. Finally, under Alexander the Great (330 BC) they enjoyed a common Hellenistic culture, in which their native heritage emerged again, and they took back their role of chemical and technical supremacy under the Roman Empire.

During the years around AD 650 the Arabs, united by Mohammed, conquered the Near East, Persia, North Africa, and most of Spain, giving to these regions a relatively homogeneous culture, in which almost all techniques were carried to a far higher point than anywhere in Europe.

These techniques derived not only from the Hellenistic and Roman dispersed knowledge, but also from India and China, with which the Arabs start to have and consolidate fruitful relationships of commerce.

The Islamic culture retained its supremacy until the thirteenth century, when the descent of the Mongols casts in terror and misery all populations and Bagdad was plundered and fired. Beside these great civilizations, an extraordinary unified culture was evolved among the islands, joining the pre-Neolithic cultures coming from the countries facing the East and West Mediterranean coasts.

Fig. 57: Distribution map of sites where pottery related with distillation have been found.

In the 5th millennium BC in the Balkans, Asia Minor and Iberian Peninsula some centres of advanced technology emerged, spreading their knowledge far beyond the sea in the Mediterranean islands, where we find many individual cultures taking advantage of a kind of silent agreement, promoting movements of people and novelties.

Many technological suggestions arrived on the Mediterranean giving birth to a form of Thalassocracy among Sardinia, Kriti, Cyprus, and almost all the Aegean islands (Fig. 57). In this colourful scenario born the Mycenaean/Greek language spoken by people who underwent a hitherto unparalleled mental development founding the principle of philosophy and theoretical science.

In chronologically competition with China, the most interesting geographical region to have an early involvement in the invention of distillation, is the East Mesopotamia crossed by the Tigris river and tributaries coming down from the Zagros mountains. An area archaeologically famous because of involvement in the Neolithic revolution that arrived on Mediterranean coasts around the 10th millennium BC (Fig. 58).

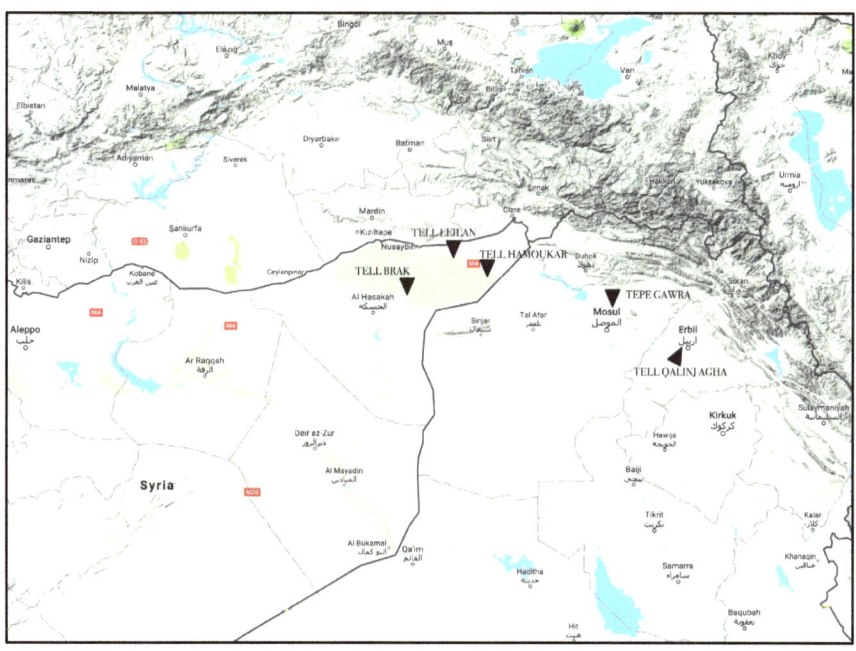

Fig. 58: Map of the Mesopotamia sites where channel pots has been found.

In this region, North East from Mosul, the ancient Nineveh capital of Sumerian Kingdom, the knowledge of distillation seems to date back the 5th millennium BC. The theory is founded on the discovery in five different sites, deep bowls, which have around the mouth two rims forming an open channel with small holes through the inside, probably pertaining to the lower part of a sort of device for distillation. Twelve specimens, four complete and eight fragmentary have been found at Tepe Gawra in Iraq, a small village of about one hectare (Fig. 59), along the Tigris valley hosting a community of 150-200 people from the 7th millennium to the 2nd millennium BC, near the actual village of Fadiliyah. Tepe Gawra comes from the Kurdish words meaning "great mound, the site is in Northern Iraq, 24 km NE of Mosul, it was discovered in 1927 by Ephraim A. Speiser[48]. In the last fifty years other sites around Tepe Gawra in the Tigris valley have been investigated and more specimens and fragments of rims fitting to the same typology have been found at Tell Qalinj Agha (Erbil), Tell Brak [49] (Fig. 60), Leilan Tepe [50] and Tell Khirbat al-Fakhar Hamoukar[51].

Fig. 59: Landscape view of Tepe Gawra.

---

[48] *Excavations at Tepe Gawra 1*, University of Pennsylvania - Museum of Archaeology and Anthropology, 1935; Arthur Tobler, *Excavations at Tepe Gawra 2*, University of Pennsylvania - Museum of Archaeology and Anthropology, 1950; M. Levey 1959. *Chemistry and Chemical Technology in Ancient Mesopotamia*, Amsterdam: Elsevier, 31-41. Sumerian Still from Tepe Gawra (ca. 3500 B.C.). (After Levey, Centaurus 4 [1955] Pl. facing, p. 24)
[49] Abu al Soof 1969:15; Oates 1987: 194
[50] Wilkinson, T. J. and D. J. Tucker 1995 Settlement Development in the North Jazira, Iraq. British School of Archaeology in Iraq. Warminster: Aris & Phillips; Khaled Abu Jayyab 2012: A ceramic chronology from Tell Hamoukar's southern extension 87-129.
[51] Khaled Abu Jayyab 2012: A Ceramic Chronology from Tell Hamoukar Southern Extension, 95. in C. Marro ed. After the Ubaid: Interpreting Change from the Caucasus

Fig. 60: Aerial view of Tell Brak large settlement.

All seem to belong to the same chronology spanning between the 4200 to 3800 BC, corresponding to the IX-XII levels of Tepe Gawra and the CH XIII of Tell Brak and LC1-2 (Late Ubaid 1-2) of Khirbat al-Fakhar Hamoukar, testifying that the channel pot of Tepe Gawra is far to be an isolated phenomenon[52], as it is generally reported in publications of the history of perfumes.

---

to Mesopotamia at the Dawn of Urban Civilization (4500-3500 BC): *Papers from* the post-Ubaid Horizon in the Fertile Crescent and Beyond, *International Workshop held at Fosseuse, 29th June-1st July 2009.* Varia Anatolica XXVII, 87-129 Paris.

[52] S. Al Quntar, L. Khalidi and J. Ur 2011: Proto-Urbanism in The Late 5th Millennium Bc: Survey and Excavations at Khirbat Al-Fakhar (Hamoukar), Northeast Syria, 157, 159, Fig. 7: 1,2,3. In: Paléorient, 2011, vol. 37, n°2. pp. 151-175: "*A distinctive large form has a wide double rim that forms a broad channel around the top of the vessel. The inner rim is usually pierced, probably for drainage of liquid from the channel into the vessel. Two versions of this pot can be distinguished. The first is crudely made with both rims at roughly the same height (fi g. 7: 1-2). The second form is burnished and in some cases slipped in black or red, with the outer rim a twice the height of the inner rim (fi g. 7: 3). In Level 3, the first form is more frequent (83.4% of examples), while the second form is more common in Level 2 (57% of total sherds of this type), a trend that continues in Level 1*".

Comparing the examples found in five sites at different levels, archaeologist Khaled Abu Jayyab[53] observes an evolution of the type, as in the earlier examples the inner rim is roughly the same height as the outer rim, while in later examples the outer rim is three times the height of the inner rim. This means that the shape was intentionally modified to improve its efficiency.

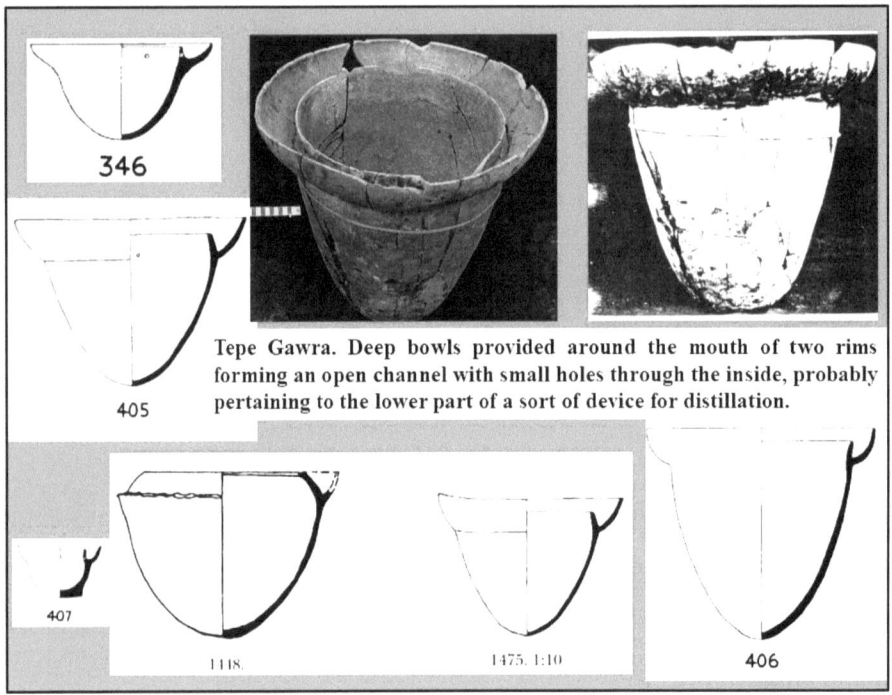

Fig. 61: 7 Specimens of the Tepe Gawra double rim pot (1:10), miniature n: 407.

Martin Levey (Pennsylvania State University), who in 1950 assembled some vases of Tepe Gawra from the fragments, recognised their function, making comparison with description of similar objects reported in Akkadian texts of the mid- 2nd millennium BC and in Muslim texts of Arab Alchemists al Razi (Abu Bakr Mohammad ibn Zakariya al Razi 864-930) and Jabir (Abu Musa Jabir ibn Hayyan al azdi 721-815), suggesting a

---

[53] Khaled Abu Jayyab 2012.

millenary management and surviving of the ancient Mesopotamia technology, in Arab Alchemy. In his research, the scholar tends to demonstrate the passage and historical continuity of the art of Mesopotamian perfume into the Arab world, returning to the issue in several papers[54]. His investigation started from the translation of some Accadian tablets which report that Tapputi-Belate Kallim, Twelfth-priestess of Muhur ilani, Limmu of Qatnu-Gardu, was the perfumer of the king, expert in making fragrances with flowers (rose?), oil and Calamus according to the technique of distillation (Fig. 62).

Fig. 62: Tapputi-Belate Kallim tablet.

---

[54] M. Levey 1960. A Group of Akkadian Texts on Perfumery: Early Muslim Chemistry: its debt to Ancient Babylonia. In *Chymia, Annual Studies in the History of Chemistry*, Vol. 6, University of Pennsylvania Press.
M. Levey 1955. Evidences of Ancient distillation, sublimation, and extraction in Mesopotamia, in *Centaurus*, 22-33.

In his book "Early Arabic Pharmacology" Levey includes some recipes and the translation of the passage mentioning the distillation procedure:

If you prepare flowers, oil, and Calamus as a salve, and you have tested the flowers [of the Calamus and its green parts], you set up... a distillery. You put good potable water ... [into a hariu pot]. You heat tabilu and put it in. You put 1 qa (about half a litre) hamimu, 1 qa iaruttu, 1 qa of good, filtered myrrh into the hariu pot.

Your standard in this is the water taken and divided. You operate at the end of the day and the evening.

It remains overnight. It becomes steeped.

You filter this solution ... with a filter cloth into a hirsu pot at dawn, on the rising of the sun. You clarify from this hirsu pot into another hirsu pot. You discard the residue. You use 3 qa of purified 'Cyperus' [species unknown] in the solution with the aromatics.

Discard the inferior material. You put 3 qa myrrh, 2 qa pressed and filtered calamus in the solution with these aromatics in a hirsu pot.

You measure 40 qa of this solution which remained overnight with the aromatics ... 1 1/2 pure gullu ... two beakers ... small beakers ... You filter ... kanaktu in a sieve.

You decant oil in the hariu pot ...in the solution.

[You rub that which was with the solution overnight.] [You examine] the comminute material. You remove [its bad part]. You filter this solution which [you clarified into a distillatory] ... 3 qa ... [You throw] ...balsam into this solution in [a hirsu pot].

[You kindle a fire]. When the solution is heated for admixture, [you pour in the oil]. You agitate with a stirrer.

*[When the oil, solution, and aromatics] continue to dissolve, [you raise]
the fire... You cover the distillatory on top.
[You cool] with [water]. When the sun [rises], [you prepare] a
[container for the oil, solution, and aromatics.
You allow the fire under the distillatory to die down.
You remove the distilled and sublimed substances from
[the trough of the distillatory ...].
When the sun [rises], [if] they continue to dissolve in one another and
[the fire rises], you cover the [top] of the distillatory. You cool.
You prepare a flask for the calamus oil. You put a filter cloth over the
flask. You filter the oil with a filter cloth into the flask. You remove
the dregs and residue left in the distillatory.
This is the preparation of flowers, oil, and calamus for [salve] the
king according to the recipe of Tapputi-Belatekallim, the perfumer,
the twentieth of Muhur-ilani, Limmu of Qatnu-gardu".*

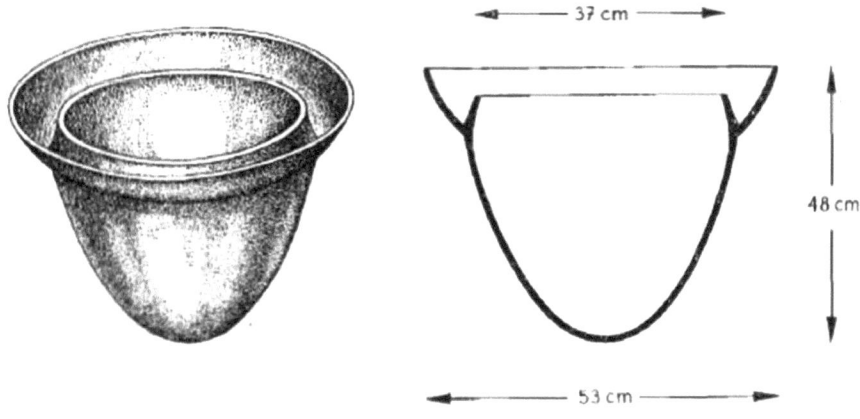

Fig. 63: Drawings of Late Ubaid type of channel pot from Rysanek & Václavû, 1989.

The twelve pots of Tepe Gawra belong to a very precise Late Ubaid typology including a miniature specimen (n° 407). All have a deep body with rounded conical bottom, which suggests the employ of a stand or contrivance of large dimensions for use on the fire. In practical terms, the vessel has a 50cm diameter mouth (medium sized) with a channel ring 8-cm thick and 10/12 deep (Fig.63), corresponding to a capacity of 37/40 litres for the pot and 2 litres for the gutter, as it is well visible in Fig. 64 (replica of the Chemicals Museum at La Sapienza of Rome). Considering that the lid is an interpretation made to give a complete appearance to the device, the size of the canal around the jar occupies a large percentage of the total height of the vase, being a sufficient room where it was possible to locate berries, resins, flowers, or crushed parts of plants to make scented waters[55].

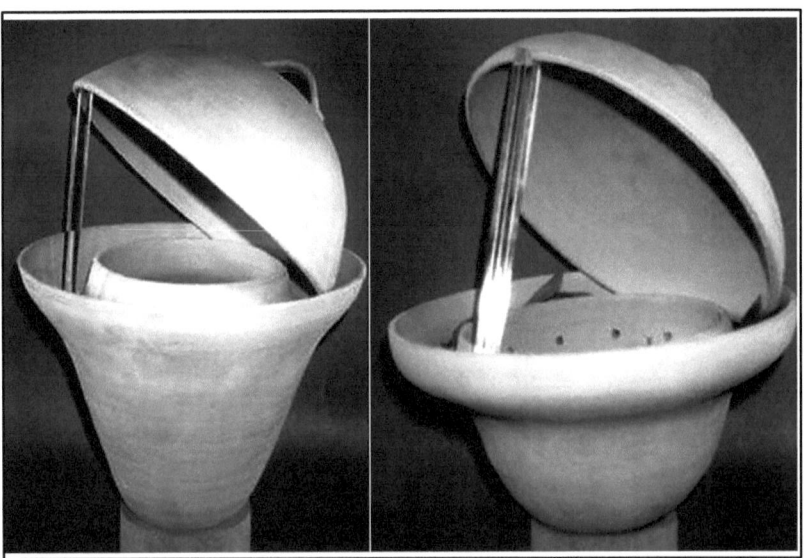

Fig. 64: Replica of the double rim Ubaid pot at the Chemicals Museum of "La Sapienza" University of Rome.

---

[55] About this I agree with Needham 1980, p. 82 fig. 1455: *"These Assyriologists also describe companion pieces having holes connecting the annular gutter with the body of the pot; such vessels were doubtless used as extractors, the plant material to be extracted being placed in the rim"*.

The miniature specimen has a flat base and given the size was probably a pottery pattern or a toy. All have holes in the inner rim which could be used to drop inside liquid possibly collecting in the mouth channel.

According to the maps of excavations, with the distribution of the artefacts, published by Mitchell Rothman, who wrote his PhD thesis on Tepe Gawra according the documentation conserved in the Pennsylvania University, most of these pots were inside the houses and positioned in one corner near benches: n. 346 level XI a square 5J[56], n. 405 level X square Q8[57], 406 level IX square 6J. Meanwhile, the miniature specimen n. 407 was part of the outfit of a grave excavated below the level XI[58] (7S, Locus G36-129).

Unfortunately, during the excavations made in the '30s by Ephraim A. Speiser and Arthur Tobler, only the intact or reconstructed vessels have been preserved and recorded, while the huge amount of ceramics found in fragments was discarded without any registration. Therefore, there may have been other vessels in the pile, as well as those associated with the function for which they were employed, in terms of pertinence to the same device or the outfit related to them.

Considering the importance given by Needham to the presence and position of the strainer in the Chinese apparatus, and the surviving of this component in modern and primitive devices producing alcoholic beverages, I searched in the inventory of the finds of Tepe Gawra

---

[56] N°. 346. H. 256, d. 496. G5-1444. XI-A, 5J. Baghdad.

[57] 405. Double-rimmed pot, gritty brown ware, dark brown wash on both surfaces, trickles of white wash on exterior; h. 365, d. 535. G6-165. XI, 8Q. 406. Double-rimmed pot, coarse brown ware, burnt black in spots; h. 480, d. 530. G3-71. IX, 6J. 33-3-36 Baghdad.

[58] 407. Miniature double-rimmed pot, hard gritty brown ware, gray slip; h. 71, d. 125. G6-326. Below XI, 7S, Locus G36-129, grave;

recordings of filter pots, or clay movable strainers, finding 7 items of different shape in five diverse levels[59].

The most interesting is n. 360[60], which has perfect dimensions (h. 33,6, d. 22,2) to be inserted inside the channel pots and hold a quantity of organic material.[61] The shape is that of an elongated oval strainer flask with a short-rounded neck and walls completely pierced. A second similar specimen was found in level X, but not illustrated because it is too fragmentary (Rothman 159).

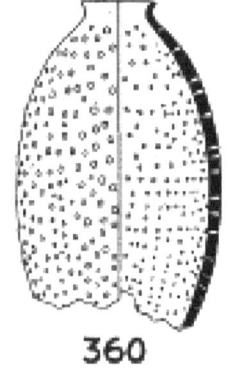

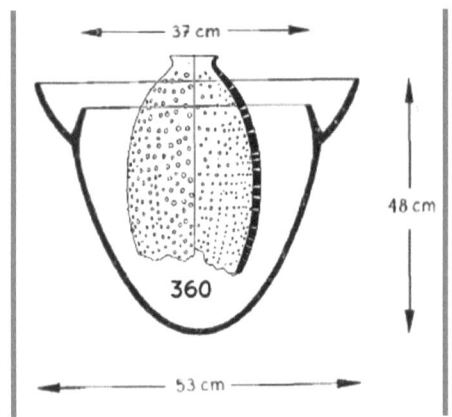

Fig. 65: Tepe Gawra channel pot n.406 (H.48xd.53) and Tepe Gawra strainer flask n° 360, H.33,6 x d. 22,2.

Except for the elongated body and the dimensions similar to the largest, the type has nothing in common with the items illustrated in chapter V from Macedonia and Indus valley (Fig. 33 and 34), even if the employ

---

[59] Please find the correspondence between the strainers and the channel pots: strainers in XI-XIAB (2), Xa (2), X (1), IX (1) and VIII (1); channel pots in XIAB 6, 4 in level XI, 1 in X, and 1 in IX.

[60] Arthur J. Tobler Excavations at Tepe Gawra, vol. II, Philadelphia 1950, 239, n. 360. Strainer, light buff ware; h. 33,6, d. 22,2. G5-1339. XI-A, 6G.

[61] Idem, p. 153, "*Fig. 360 is a specialized type of strainer; why such a form was required, and to what precise purpose it was applied is speculative*".

could be the same. Ann Harman (2015) in her book Harvest to Hydrosol[62] describes clearly the difference among *hydro-distillation with plant material in water, steam distillation with plant material above water, wet steam distillation with plant material on screen above water*, and *hydro/steam combination with plant material both in water and above water.* What is interesting about the drawings she published to explain the differences, is the presence in one of a column element superimposed to the pot, holding the plants to be processed that suggests the correct use of the elongated cylindrical or oval flask strainers (Fig. 66).

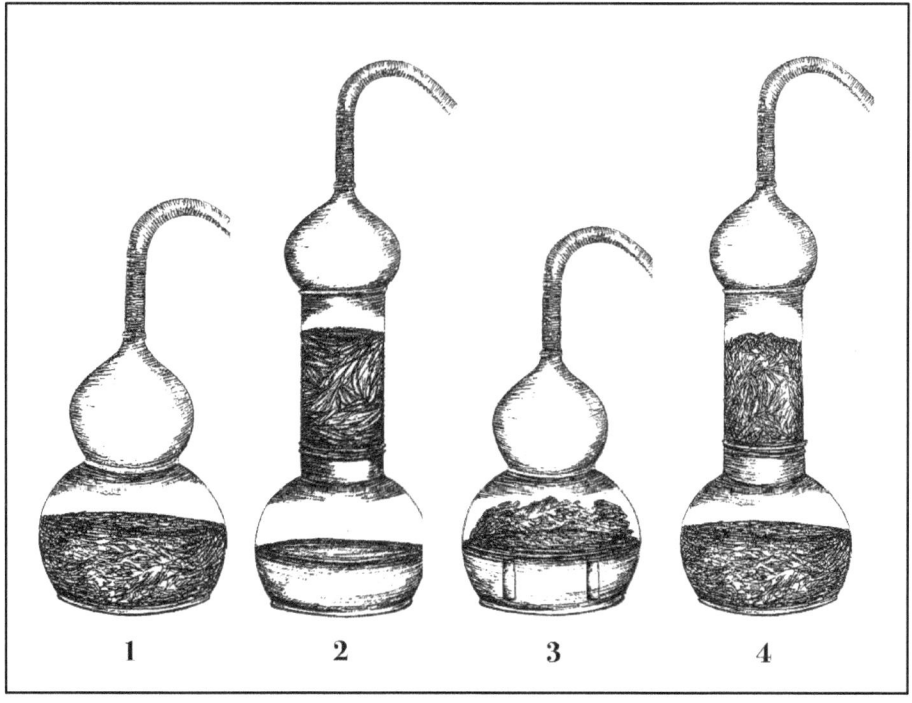

Fig. 66: 1. Hydro-distillation: plant material in water; 2. Steam-distillation: plant material above water; 3. Wet steam distillation: plant material on screen above water; 4. Hydro/steam combination: plant material both in water and above water.
From Harman 2015, Figure 3. 1,2,3,4.

---

[62] Harman A. 2015: Harvest to Hydrosol, IAG Botanics LLC dba bot AN Nicals Fruitland, WA 99129. 43-50.

Regarding the funnels, we have an intriguing description of Tobler[63]: *"Wide funnels with curved sides are introduced in Stratum XII-A, but first become common in XII. Fig. 320[64] is representative of several more, some of which had their interiors covered with bitumen. The series of piercings ringing the bottom of fig. 319 [65] is an unusual feature, while an even more unconventional specimen is illustrated in fig. 325[66]. The deep bell-shape of this object and its small opening near the rim are details which are unduplicated on other funnels".*

Fig. 67: Funnel pots from Stratum XII-XII-A of Tepe Gawra, Tobler 1950: Fig. 319, Fig. 320, and Fig. 325.

His short note is quite important as it informs us of the presence of a different kind of object, with an unusual form halfway between a funnel and a strainer, suggesting the existence of more pottery which may have had some relations with the function of the channel bowls. The comparison with some strainers found at Troy and in Slovakia whose shape also

---

[63] Idem, p. 151.
[64] Idem, p. 238, n.320 Funnel, no description; h. 12,0, d. 33,2. G41230. XII, SM. Discarded.
[65] Idem, p. 238, n. 319 Funnel, buff ware; h. 7,5, d. 24,2. G6-72. Below XII, 6M.
[66] Tobler, p. 239, n. 325. Funnel, coarse light brown ware; h. 22,0, d. 22,8. G5-1665. XII, 4-0.

appears as a fusion between funnel and filter[67], seems to justify their presence at Tepe Gawra.

Of course, the flask strainer whose shape is quite different from the Circum-Mediterranean examples, does not help in recognising the material processed, only suggesting it belongs to a steam distillation that requires the use of a strainer, for extracting essences letting the steam pass through[68]. The same function had the channel added on the vessel edge.

However, the funnel pots, could have been employed in distillation, especially n.325[69] (Fig.67), a sort of large bell-shaped funnel, provided with a hole in the bottom and on the side (Fig.67), where it was possible to insert bamboo canes. And the n° 320[70] catalogued as a funnel because it is a bowl with a large open base, without any spout, found with the remains of blackish burned resin identified as bitumen. Sadly, in Tobler's recording we read that this object was discarded because it was considered a matter of no importance. Waiting for more information from archaeometry investigation, which are still possible as many vases are preserved in the Penn Museum of the Pennsylvania University, which at the time sponsored the excavations taking the 50% of the findings (see Penn Museum web site); my opinion on the addressing of these vases is for making perfumed waters. Considering the exceptional number of channel pots found at Tepe Gawra and around, their production is a unique event in the history of distillation including their curated position inside

---

[67] Carinci F., 2011. "Strumentazione per il filtraggio nei contesti di apparato del primo palazzo di Festòs", in Kretes Minoikos. Studi offerti a Vincenzo La Rosa per il suo 70°compleanno, Studi di archeologia cretese, X. Bottega d'Erasmo, A. Ausilio: Padova, pp.103-115.
[68] Ann Harman 2015, 43-50.
[69] Tobler, 1950: p. 239: Catalogue n°. 325:" Funnel, coarse light brown ware, wet-smoothed; l. 225, h.143. G6-392. Below XII, 6G. Bagdad Museum. Pl. CXXXII, 325.
[70] Tobler 1950: n° 320 (p. 238) Funnel, no description; h.120, d.332. G4-1230. XII, 5M. Discarded. Pl. CXXXII, 320.

the houses, and the relative minor number of people (150/200) inhabiting the small village, the twelve channel pots testify the presence of a specialized activity in producing something that enriched the whole community. Indeed, many more are supposed since fragments were previously discarded. This is indirectly confirmed by Mitchell Rothman who, republishing Tepe Gawra material, underlines the extraordinary number of luxuries collected (incised seals and sealings and jewels including gold and silver), suggesting the small community produced something special or precious in order to become so rich.

He points to the textiles mentioning the number of spindle whorls found and the presence of silver and gold items in the graves. But, the insignificant number of loom weights found in different levels (12 small fragments in total) points to exclude the manufacture of precious clothes.

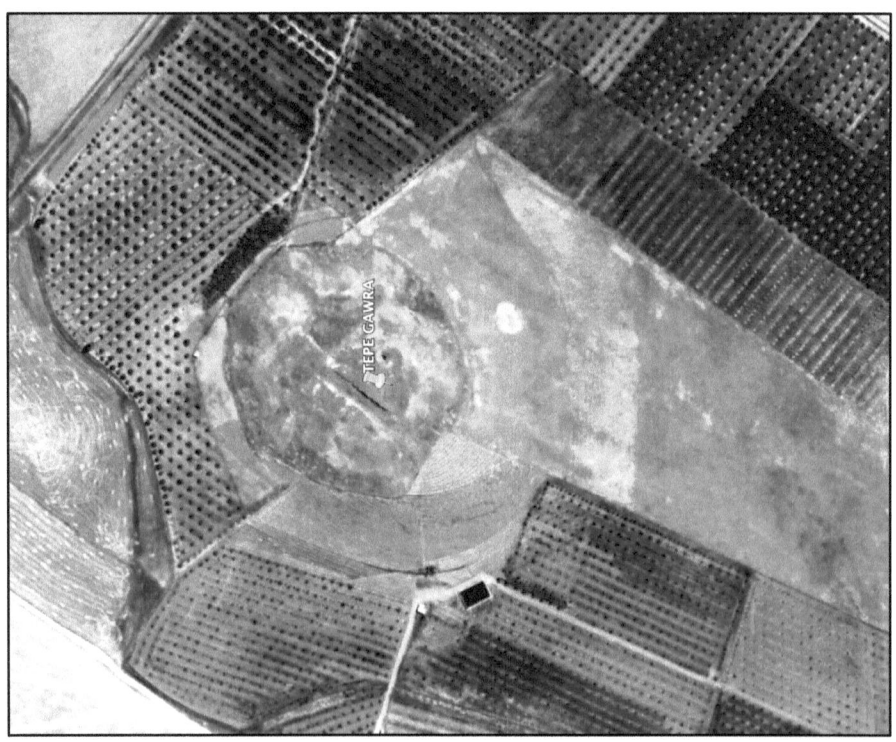

Fig. 68: Aerial view of Tepe Gawra hill: still visible are central soundings cutting the top and the limits of occupation.

Meanwhile the production of perfumed waters, probably relating to the tripartite temple located in the middle of the village, seems a more reliable suggestion even considering that the same devices were used in the same period by other communities living in the upper Tigris valley.

Thus, confirming the insight of Martin Levey, and justifying the unusual wealth of the site.

In this regard, the presence of a miniature channel pot in a grave may have some meaning associated to the making of the perfumes or instead to a person (priestess) who had some role with its making and functionality.

This suggests a form of symbolic reference or special consideration of the channel pot (for the peculiarity of its invention or for its use).

Nevertheless, since the lack of information on the lost pottery repertoire, found in fragments, and discarded, we cannot reconstruct how such a workshop could have been organised to address this peculiar production.

Besides, the predominant presence of worship areas in a site whose surface does not exceed one hectare, suggests the possibility that this activity was connected in some manner with the ceremonies performed in the tripartite temple, like producing perfumes for the pilgrims and worshippers.

Worship was certainly present in the IV millennium BC, in the *country between the two rivers = Meso-potamià*, under the Sumerian supremacy and later under the Akkadian. Here, we find a complex female divinity with androgynous characters, very different from the primitive mother goddess, known as *Inanna (Akkadian) Ishtar* [71](Fig. 69).

---

[71] P. Friedrich 1982. *The Meaning of Aphrodite,* The University of Chicago Press.

The holy city was probably Uruk[72], where the sacred area with the temple of the goddess was found. However, the places of worship dedicated to her were distributed everywhere, throughout all the Sumerian kingdom.

Fig. 69: Clay relief panel representing Ishtar, 1800BC.
Courtesy British Museum, London.

Inanna was a divinity, far away from the concept of female fertility or parturient-mother. She was a female entity that enclosed in her the idea of absolute beauty and sensuality. She was associated with the planet Venus and considered sister or daughter of the sun, the Lady of sky, the star of the evening; glowing for clothes and jewellery.

To Inanna, around 2300 BC, Enheduanna the daughter of Sargon I, King of the Sumerians dedicated the first verses in poetry remembered in history[73]. In her verses, she designed a clear portrait of the divinity and of

---

[72] M. Liverani 2006. *Uruk la prima città*, Laterza, Roma.
[73] Enheduanna wrote her poetry very early in the evolution of writing, perhaps three hundred years after cuneiform vocabulary developed sufficiently to handle linguistic

her personality, in which we can recognize some characters of Aphrodite including her predilection for perfumes. Many scholars believe that from this Mesopotamian goddess the Cypriot Aphrodite comes, as she has the same attributes and astrological identifications. In the Semitic version, Inanna was then identified with Ishtar, with more pronounced features that make her very like the Cypriot divinity. The presence of prostitute priestess's in the temples and places of worship dedicated to the deity is intriguing. Here precious perfumes and ointments were produced and used during the ritual. The Tepe Gawra apparatus has been reconstructed with an imaginary cover with two unlikely ears/handles[74](Fig. 70), which have no comparison with any of the clay ceramics found on the site. With the pottery repertoire published by Ephraim A. Speiser (1935), James Arthur Tobler and Mitchell S. Rothman, as well as other published material, it is possible to speculate different solutions concerning the top of the channel pots are from being sublimation devices.

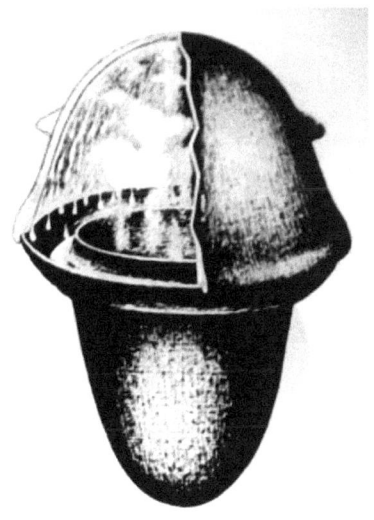

Fig.70: Reconstruction of Tepe Gawra apparatus of Rysanek & Václavû, 1989.

---

concepts": J. Grahan 2000. Foreword in Betty De Shong Meador, Lady of Largest Heart: poems of the Sumerian high priestess Enheduanna, University of Texas Press.
[74] Rysanek & Václavû, 1989, fig. 3, p. 199

Among the repertoire of Tepe Gawra a spouted pot (Fig. 71) was found in level IX (spout fragmentary, preserved only the half: Tobler inv. N° 411, Pl. CXLVII (Rothman n° 2233; 3-137 33-3-63 level IX, red brown ware

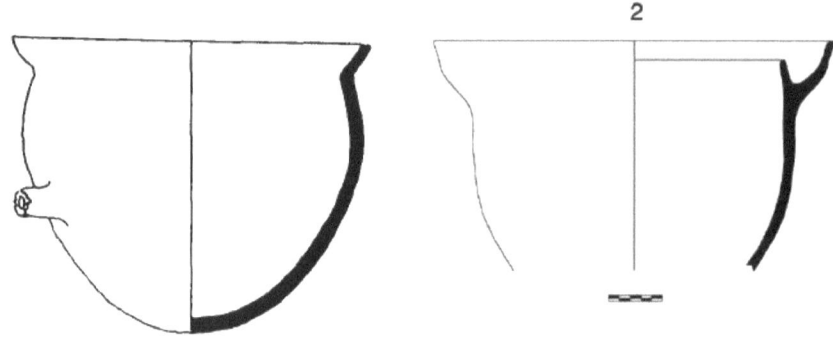

Fig. 71: Spouted jar from Tepe Gawra and channel pot from Tell Hammoukar.

9K 80, H. 30,3cm, rim D. 38 cm)[75], which may represent an interesting possibility, not only because it is spouted, but for the intriguing case it has the same shape and mouth diameter of a channel pot found at Tell Hammoukar[76] (Fig. 71). Such a similarity suggests it may have been made by the same artisan[77]. Moreover, as the max. diameter of T.G. n. 2233 is 38cm it is possible to use it as a head on three pots from Tepe Gawra with the inside rim of 37 cm, and on other fragmentary specimens which seem to have the same dimension of the Tell Hammoukar channel pot. In the case of Tepe Gawra n. 406 (inside rim 37 cm) under Tepe Gawra n.2233 we obtain an interesting device which take advantage both of a channel

---

[75] Rothman M.J. 2000: *Tepe Gawra: The evolution of a small, prehistoric center in Northern Iraq.* 55, 59, 256, 273, 376, pl. 20.
[76] Khaled ABU Jayyab 2012: Fig. 10: LC 2 Jars level 1, n° 2.
[77] Many other spouted pots and crock are mentioned in the inventory list of M. Rothman, for some of them the dimension and drawings are reported even if the pot was discarded, while n.2233 is in Penn Museum inv. n. 33-3-063.

rim to recover the dripping coming down from the walls (enriching the result), and a side spout to collect the condensation (Fig.72).

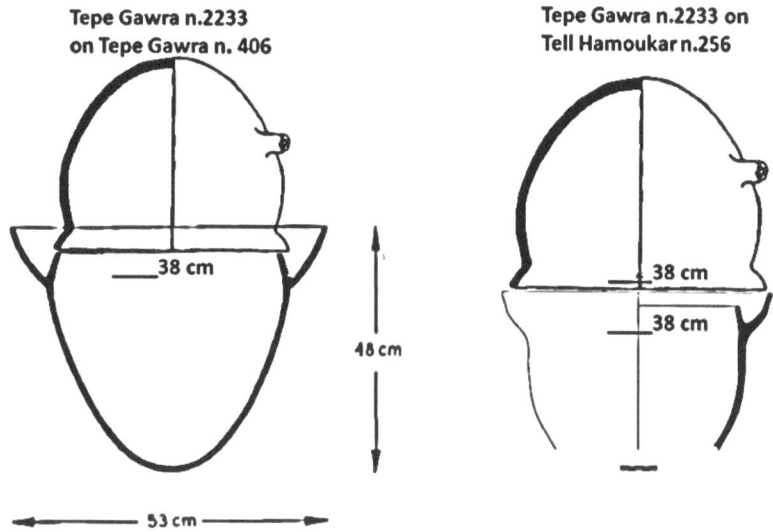

Fig. 72: Experimental assemblage of T.G. n°2233 on T.G. n° 406 and T.G. n°2233 on T. H.

The assemblage of the two pots (Tepe Gawra on Tell Hammoukar), for which we have only drawings, is only virtual. A combination, however, is more realistic than the graphic reconstruction proposed by Rysanek & Václavû.[78] The pots together form a normal still apparatus, giving reason for the channel/strainer that holds the plants to be distilled and to the spout of the "cover" to collect the water distilled.

The high volumetric capacity of the vase, around 40 litres, is unsuitable for sublimation process[79] supporting the hypothesis that it was used for distillation of alcoholic beverages or scented waters.

---

[78] Rysanek & Václavû, 1989, fig. 3, p. 199
[79] Unthinkable at the beginning of the fourth millennium BC.

Considering also the small extension of the village, the minor number of inhabitants and the fact that the channel pots were in domestic contexts, the possibility that they were used for sublimation processes of inorganic materials seems very remote. While, domestic production of alcoholic beverages or scented waters is beyond the Mesopotamian scenario rebuilt by Marc Levey. Unfortunately, until the recently the practical ignorance of the distillation systems employed (around the world) to produce spirits, perfumed waters, and chemical components made it difficult to recognize dismantled parts of ancient distillation apparatuses composed of simple pots and assembled on bench/ furnaces, such as the Tepe Gawra case.

♍

The Tepe Gawra apparatus with its "imaginary cover" has been reconstructed many times and compare with later alchemical equipment. Replicas are on display at the Museum of Chemistry of the University La Sapienza of Rome in Italy, at the Jagiellonian University Museum of Pharmacy of Krakow in Poland and at the Museum of Alchemists and Magicians of old Prague in Czechoslovakia.

X. From Anatolia to Slovakia, Sardinia, and Cyprus

Taking aside Mesopotamia and its channel pots for comparison, we move around the Mediterranean to find more evidence that suggests these devices were not an isolated phenomenon. Nor the product of a local technological background belonging to a rare but specific wisdom (Fig. 73).

The first class of objects by date and proximity are some intriguing Hittite modified pitchers of the 2nd millennium BC, found nearby cult places and in funerary context. One of these specimens, conserved in the *Bogazkoy Museum, Bogaskale, Turkey* has been recently investigated by J. Bartholomew (2015). Bartholomew made a replica of the vase as well as experiments of distillation with it, presenting the results at the Conference 'Creativity and Craft Production in Middle and Late Bronze Age Europe' (10 – 11 April 2013. Magdalen College, Cambridge), including comparisons with Tepe Gawra and fragmentary strainers from Troy, Slovakia, and Hungary.

The photo and drawings he published were from the showcase of the Bogazkoy Museum, reporting brief description of the object found in the excavation of Hattusa, and identified a as cult vessel. In terms of typology the pot is a sort of fake teapot; it has an inner inverted funnel running inside from the base thus creating a collecting collar likely for the gathering of condensation vapour rising from below[80].

---

[80] Fischer F. 1963: Die Hethitische Keramik von Bogazkoy, Berlin

Fig. 73: Channel strainers and pots distribution from Anatolia to Slovakia.

The vase does not have a neck but only a spout pointing up, the top shaped like a dome hosts a coroplastic group composed by two figurines representing a ram introduced by a naked man, probably symbolizing a religious ceremony or sacrifice. Opposite the spout (ending with a sort of cutaway duck head) there is a vertical basket handle (missing).

The base looks similar to a stump foot, hiding the short-enlarged neck of the funnel. The pot it is not unique, as it belongs to a specific type of Hittite "cult vase" of the beginning of the second millennium BC found also at Eskiyapar, Alacahoyuk (20km from) and Ferzant (all with the collecting collar inside, in exhibition at the Museum of Anatolian

Civilizations, Ankara)[81]. One of the specimens in the exhibition (Fig. 74) has been restored with red and black fragments suggesting prior to breaking, the pot suffered a direct contact with the fire, probably during its use.

Fig. 74: Fake teapots from Hattusa, and Eskiyapar.
Museum of Anatolian Civilizations. Ankara.

---

[81] Fischer, F., Die hethitische Keramik von Boğazköy. Boğazköy-Hattuša 4 (Berlin 1963), 123 Nr. 346 Taf. 32. 346; Özgüç, T., "Vases used for ritual purposes from Eskiyapar" T. Mikasa (ed.), Essays on Ancient Anatolia. Bulletin of the Middle Eastern Culture Center in Japan (Wiesbaden 1999) 1-23, s. 4-5 Pl. 8a; Recke, M., "Eine Trickvase von der Akropolis in Perge und andere Zeugnisse für kultische Aktivitäten während der Mittel- und Spätbronzezeit: Zur Rolle Pamphyliens im 2. Jahrtausend v. Chr." A. Erkanal-Öktü v.d. (ed.), Hayat Erkanal'a Armağan. Kültürlerin Yansıması (İstanbul 2006) 618-626, s. 618-620, Abb. 1; 3; 7-8; Martini, W., Die Akropolis von Perge in Pamphylien – vom Siedlungsplatz zur Akropolis (Stuttgart 2010), 16-19, Abb. 6a-b.

In a similar condition, we found the alembics at Pyrgos, overwhelmed by adjacent structures when the fire under them or nearby was still active (Fig. 116, Fig. 117). This suggests that the incident happened while the device was functioning. The two specimens from Eskiyapar, found together in the Level VI, c (corresponding to the first phase of the Old Hittite period) are approximately the same size as the item from Hattusa.

Although they, diverging in some details; one has a pointed conical dome and the second has the dome shaped like a fake lid, and a tape handle positioned not opposite the spout but on the side. It looks as though it is made to appear as a normal stumped mug in order to better hide its real use and contents.

As illustrated by Needham, the dynamic process that this instrumental pot could carry out is fairly clear[82] if we consider it the top of a still apparatus composed of expansion vase and having no boiler, in this case working also as a collector (Fig. 75).

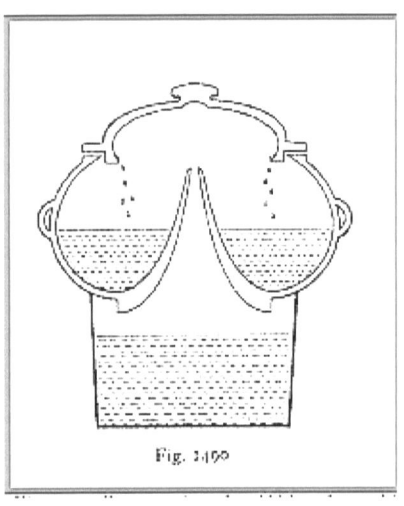

Fig. 75: Dynamic process illustrated by Needham 1980: p. 116, Fig. 1490, and the experimental reconstruction of Bartholomew.

---

[82] Needham 1980: p. 116, Fig. 1490.

J. Bartholomew's experiment employed a simple jar of a medium size, practically showing the easy and correct functionality of the object that in its complicated simplicity, proves to be an artefact born in a rich and evolved environment. It has collected technical and cultural suggestions from Mesopotamia palatial civilizations within which there were continuous traffics through the millennial caravan road crossing central Anatolia and continuing towards the Balkans and Eastern Europe.

The vase is of some importance in the history of distillation as it is the first artefact which includes all the components of what will be recognised after 3000 years, as the functional peculiarities of the alembic, or "capitello", or dome head of the glass distiller (chapter VII): **Dome, Spout, Channel (collecting collar), and Neck**.

Besides, we should remember that these components are typologically present in almost all the Mediterranean vascular repertoires since the beginning of Bronze age. The main peculiarity of the distiller is that the liquid collected could remain inside the pot until its employment, confirming a possible exclusive and religious destination of the device.

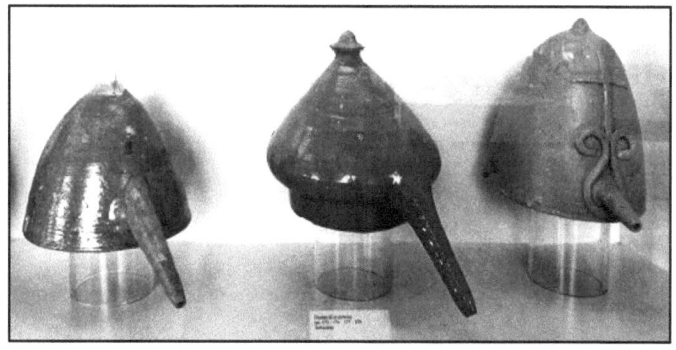

Fig. 76: Clay Alembic heads 15th and 16th century at Alembic Museum of Gubbio, Italy and at London Museum.

The Hittite type seems to have had a personal success spreading to Central Europe throughout an unknown historical path, as we have comparisons dating to the XV and XVI centuries, including England and Italy[83] (Fig. 76).They have the characteristic conical shape of the head with an internal collecting collar which could be considered a Renaissance variant of the round dome version if these specimens did not testify to the surviving and evolution of the type during the long history of distillation (Fig.77). Although the idea of making a second rim inside of a pot to create an additional extra space brings us back to Tepe Gawra. However, the use is completely different; Tepe Gawra collar works like a strainer-container whereas at Hattusa it is a colleting collar.

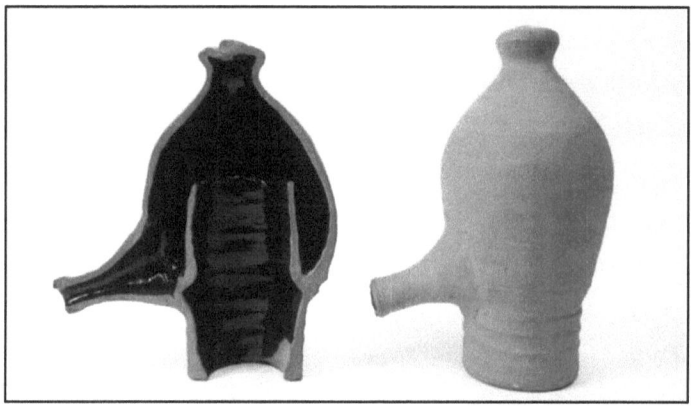

Fig. 77: Didactic illustration of a Tudor (Henry VIII) Alembic

Meanwhile, in Anatolia we find specimens half way between a funnel and a filter which suggests a widespread knowledge of the possible employ of detached strainer-collecting collars.

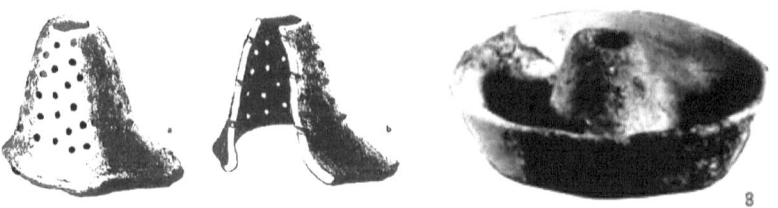

Fig. 78: Strainer component found by Schlieman at Troy 2° millenium BC, and its conservation.

---

[83] Moorhouse, S.: 1972 Fig. 31.

For instance, the funnel strainer found at Troy (Fig. 78), level V (Schliemann H. 1881, s. 643, n. 1303), has forerunners at Vrbového and Nitriansky Hrádok in Slovakia[84] dating back to between the 3rd and 4th millennium BC. These in turn compare with a more ancient strainer bowl of 5th millennium BC from Halka Bunar in Central Bulgaria district of Stara Zagora[85].

All these objects seem to be movable accessories belonging to a device, or part of a steamer, to be inserted in the middle of two pots, to perform a precise function.

Fig. 79: Double rim pot from Spišský Stvrtok Slovakia and Ryšánek & Václavů reconstruction 1989.

From Spišský Stvrtok Slovakia comes also an interesting later comparison (Fig. 79) of a double rim spouted pot, 1500 BC, which suggests a long story of survival and diffusion of the ancient technology

---

[84] Nemejcová-Pavúková, V. 1979: Nálezy bolerázskej skupiny z Vrbového. Archeol. rozhl., 31, s. 393.
[85] Ryšánek J. & V. Václavů 1989: Destilační přítroj ze spišského štrvtku, Archeologické Rozhledy, vol. 41, pp. 196-201. Ryšánek J. 1993: Extrakční přístroj z Tróje, Archeologické Rozhledy, vol. 45, pp. 127-133.

born in Mesopotamia in the 4th millennium BC[86]. However, the vessel is completely different from the type of Tepe Gawra as it has the flat base, an ovoid body with a cylindrical straight edge and a second rim added outside to form the collecting collar converging with the large beaked spout.

The same imaginary top cover of Tepe Gawra channel pot has been employed by Ryšánek & Václavů to make a graphic reconstruction of this specimen, with the assumption that the double rim with beaked spout of the pot worked as a collecting collar for the liquid dripping down in a bowl positioned below (Fig. 79).

The suggested reconstruction seems a bit simplistic, in fact, it is quite unlikely that the bowl used for gathering the liquid would be at the foot of the pot if it was on the fire. Probably the apparatus was much more complex when set up. The flat base of the jar suggests that the vessel was not on a stand, nor in direct contact with the fire. It may have been placed in a special structure, or on a bench, built on a heat source, which in turn was supporting the different parts of the apparatus. Thus, the specimen appears very different from Tepe Gawra example, with a completely different use of the channel provided with a spout for the external recovery of the distillate.

Almost in the same period, probably a result of trading spreading cultural suggestions throughout the Mediterranean (Fig. 80), we find a similar solution in Cyprus, the island that together with Sardinia was deeply involved in copper trade and production in the second half of the Late Bronze Age.

---

[86] J. Ryšánek - V. Václavů: 1989, Destilační přítroj ze spišského štrvtku, Archeologické Rozhledy, vol. 41, pp. 196-201.

In Cyprus, we find the collecting collar with a beaked spout like the Spišský Štvrtok specimen applied on a tripod pot from a tomb of the Late Bronze age from Paphos Teratsoudhia cemetery (Fig. 81).

Fig. 80: Mediterranean trades during the Late Bronze age.

The craftsman who created this pot seems to have known in some manner the Slovakian type, as he has emphasized the structural elements of the cylindrical neck and the beaked spout, confirming the dating of the Slovak example which should be older. Unlike the Slovak's, the tripod pot has two opposite ring handles positioned on the rims of the channel[87].

The specimen is similar to the tripod cooking pot made of coarse ware, and has been restored from fragments. It seems to have been part of a device composed by two pots: the lower to put straight on the fire and, the upper a simple beaked spout bowl, which is a common type of Cyprus

---

[87] V. Karageorghis 1990. Tombs at Palaepaphos, Nicosia, 66-7, Pl. XXIX, 207. - ibidem, about the fragments of a specimen from Tiryns, Fig.10.

repertoire, dropping the condensation in the collecting collar. It is evident that the ceramist who made this vessel worked far from the typological schemes, smartly assembling elements belonging to traditional cooking systems, to make a more functional contrivance.

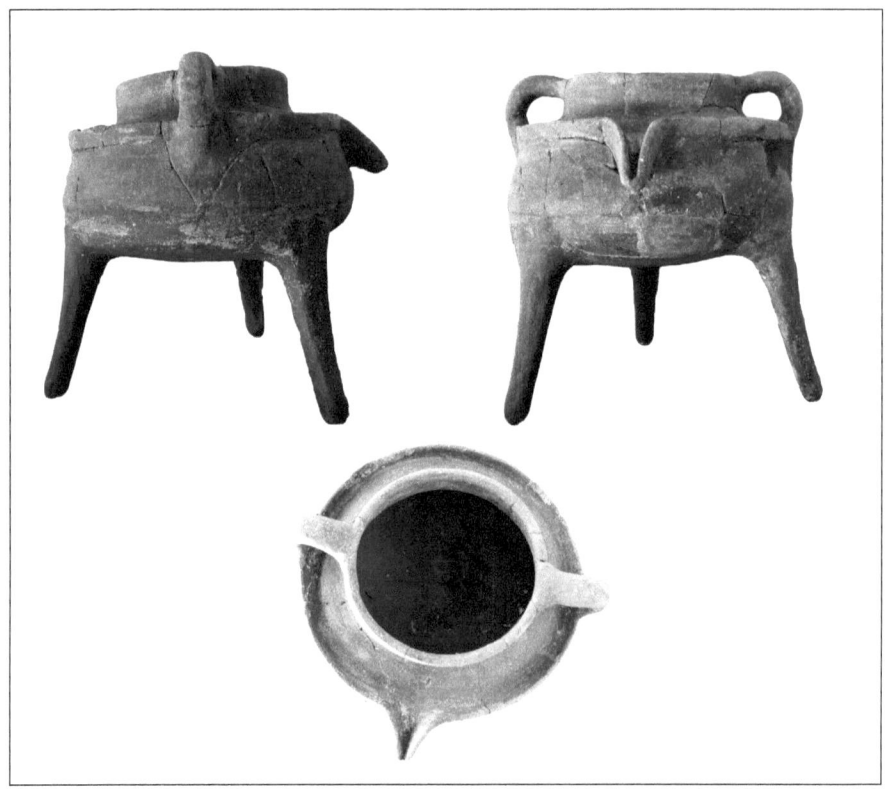

Fig. 81: Tripod from Paphos/Teratsoudhia, 1400-1500 BC, Kouklia Museum, Cyprus

The importance of this pot consists not only in the intriguing shape which represents an interesting evolution for using the collecting collar, but also because it was part of the same funerary outfit as the miniature double rim specimen found in a grave of Tepe Gawra (p.101). Generally, the cooking pots are not part of the goods positioned in a tomb so this case it may indicate that this pot was considered a precious object to honour or identify the buried person.

The same typology seems to belong to two pots from Sardinia from the Late Bronze age, found in two different Nuraghe villages. From Tertenia (Nuoro), Nuraghe Nastasi[88] comes a large pot found together with other cooking pots and stands for fire (Fig. 82a).

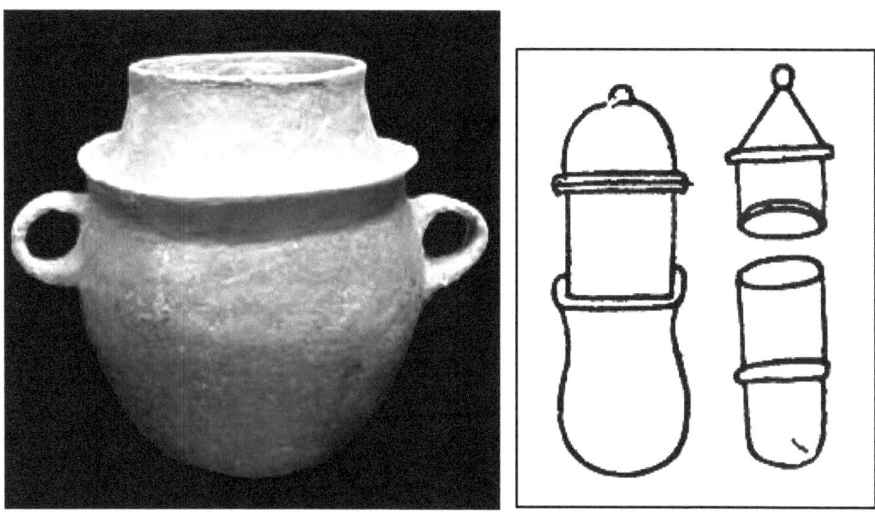

Fig. 82: a-Nuraghe Nastasi of Tertenia (1400-1000 BC), Museum G.A. Sanna, Sassari. b. *Bibliotheca Chemica* de Manget (t. I, p. 540, fig. 2 — Genève, 1702).

The vase has a rounded body with two opposite ring handles, and like the Cypriot specimen the collar is shaped by a high cylinder tapered on the top and an outer shorter rim applied on the shoulder over the handles.

Personally, I'm quite perplexed when considering this vase as part of an apparatus for distilling as the collar is missing the holes that allow the liquid to get back inside the vase. So, the only function it could have had is the collection of a small quantity of the essential oil overflowing beyond the rim of the vase. Perhaps, it is more likely it has been used for sublimation as the comparison with the schematic drawing published in the Bibliotheca Chemica de Manget let us suppose (Fig.82 b).

---

[88] Campus F. & Leonelli V.: 2000, 518, 601.

Completely different is the case of the pot from La Prisgiona (Capichera) near Arzachena, whose collar is provided with liquid return holes (Fig. 83)[89].

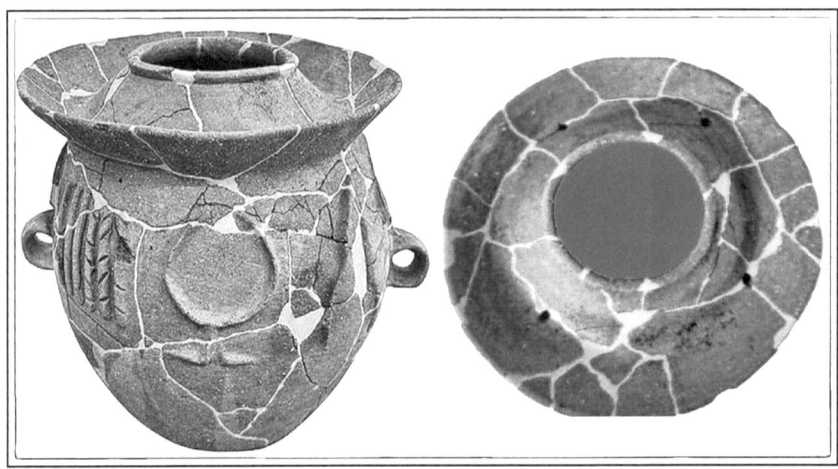

Fig. 83: Double handles jar with large holed collar, La Prisgiona (Capichera) Sardinia.

The shape of the body is ovoid until the mouth, with a small turned rim. The second flaring rim is positioned on the shoulder of the vase around the tapering mouth, raising to the level of the mouth. The vase is 50 cm high and has a fine plastic decoration applied around the body, consisting of a row of rope vertical elements, open circles and snake remnant alchemical symbols, suggesting it was employed to make some ceremonial liquid. In this case the second rim appears as an applied plastic solution for transforming a normal hole jar in a vase for special use, with ring side handles, positioned on the middle body as in the specimen from Tertenia and from Cyprus.

---

[89] Antona A., Corro M. D. M., Puggioni S. 2010: Spazi di lavoro e attività produttive nel villaggio nuragico La Prisgiona in località Capichera (Arzachena), in M. Milanese, Ruggeri P., Vismara C. ed. *L'Africa Romana. I luoghi e le forme dei mestieri e della produzione nelle province africane*. Atti del XVIII Convegno di studio Olbia 11-14 dicembre 2008. Vol. III. 1713-1734. Fig. 14. Carocci, Roma.

XI. Aegean.

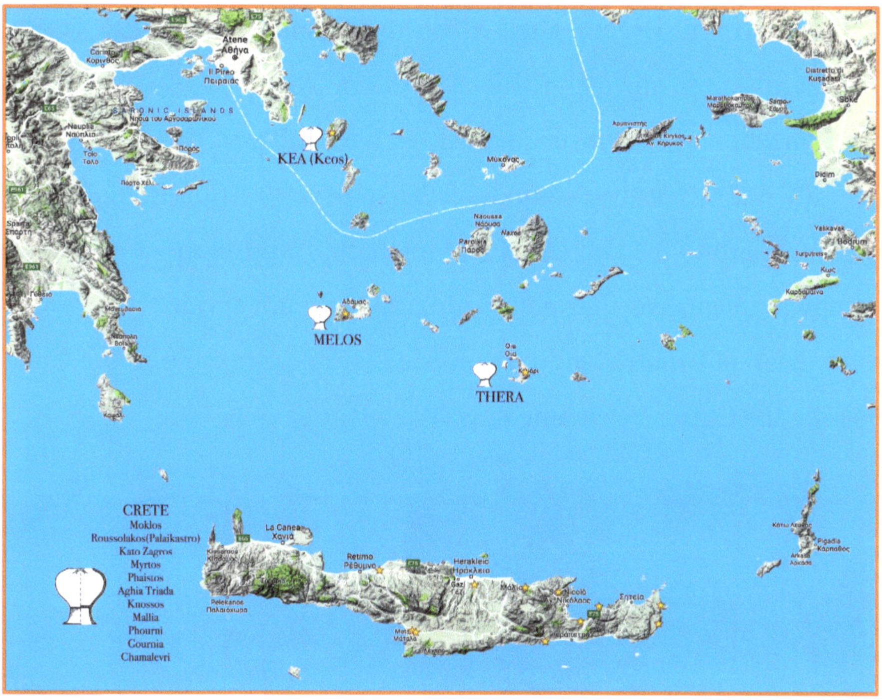

Fig. 84: Map of the major sites that have returned specimens of tureen shaped strainer.

Towards the beginning of the second millennium BC, commercial and cultural exchanges along the caravan roads of the territories surrounding the Eastern Mediterranean progressively moved more and more along the coasts, where navigation had become a safer means of transport, far from internal territorial disputes. As a result, it was possible to shorten travels and freight transport considerably. So, great commercial ports along the coasts of North Africa, the Near East and Anatolia were born, while in the Aegean Sea occupied by a myriad of large and small islands, the fervour, and the increase in traffics between the Anatolian and Greek opposite banks created not only a material wealth but also an explosion of culture that has few comparisons in antiquity.

The most sophisticated craftsmanship for metal, stone, fabric, and multi-coloured painting from the four cardinal points met and fused in the heart of the Aegean, generating one of the richest and most organized civilizations of the Bronze Age, with its own administrative systems, laws, and playful and scenic competitions.

A civilization to which scholars have given different names, but which was only one, where we should not be surprised to find intriguing clay objects regarding the subject of our research. In this second millennium BC environment, we find pots with strainers built inside[90], the type of which does not match any circum-Mediterranean example, but recalls absurdly the Chinese steaming pots (Fig.53)

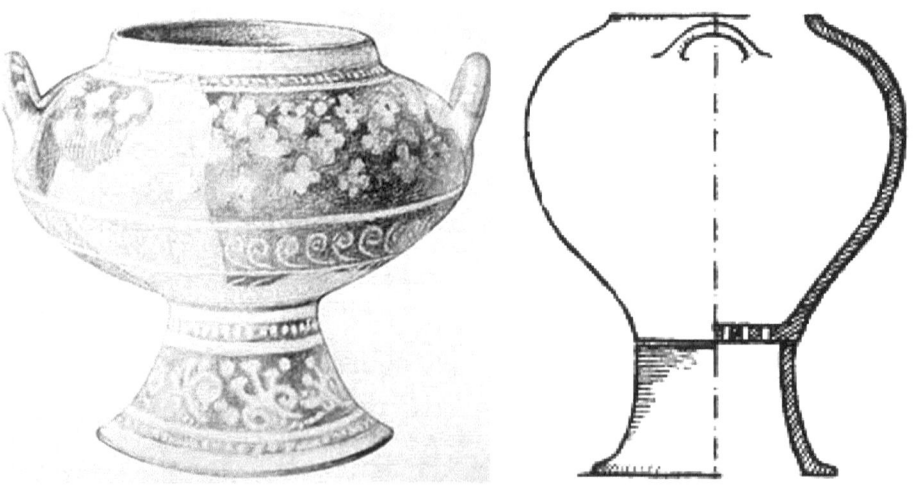

Fig. 85: LM-I-Strainer-Block-B-Mochlos AJA 13 1909 282 Pl VII.

The number of registered examples is several dozen, including specimens of small, medium and large size, found mostly in Crete, Thera (Santorini), Keos and Melos (Fig. 85). The type appears in the Middle

---

[90] Carinci, 2011.

Minoan [91] and has a precise evolution and diffusion until the end of the Mycenaean period (Fig. 84).

In 1904 Campbell Cowan Edgar suggested a Cretan origin for the type, anticipating the discovery in the Palace of Phaistos of the prototypes of this peculiar vase dating back between the 2000-1800 BC (below Fig. 86).

The two versions, (a) and (b), found in the Palace of Phaistos are quite different from one another: one (a) for the cylindrical shape has curved shoulders which anticipate the rounded body of the later pot, the second (b) has a bulbous strainer inside and a stumped base which forestalls the bell shape of the later foot. The strainer, which is the component that transforms a normal pot in an instrumental device, has a different shape and position in each version. In (a) it consists of a drilled slab positioned as a diaphragm in the middle of the vase. In (b) the strainer consists of an elongated drilled bulb rising inside from the base.

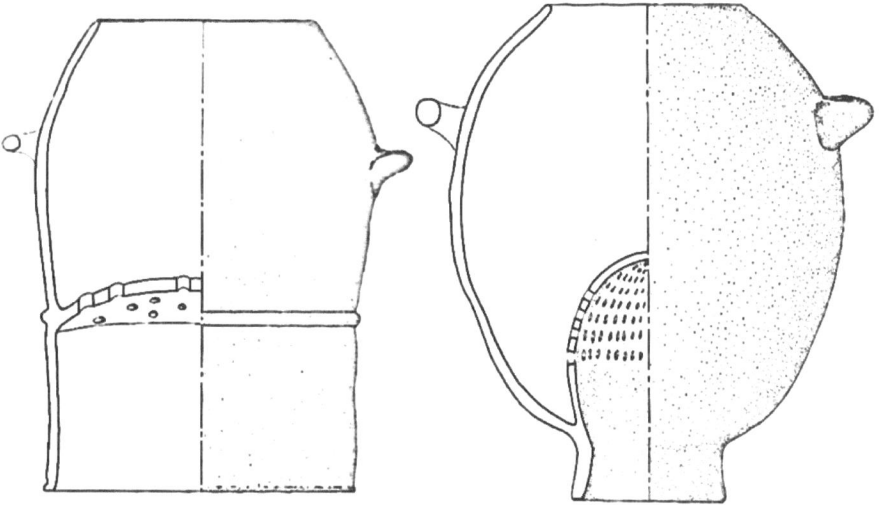

Fig. 86: Drawings of Phaistos version (a) n°1038 and (b) n° 526: from Carinci 2011.

---

[91] Campbell Cowan Edgar in 1904 suggested the type has Cretan origins. Edgar C.C. 1904 in Atkinson *et al.* 128, pl. XXIV, n. 2., referring the specimen from Kato Zakros village.

Type (a) has a cylindrical shape with a rounded upper part and a straight lower part, divided by an external rib corresponding to the internal diaphragm. Type (b) has an oval shaped body in a short conical trunk stumped base, supporting inside the strainer bulb. It seems an almost exclusive Cretan product of MMII, which did not evolve in later specimens like it. However, cylindrical strainers have been known in the Aegean environment since the Neolithic period (Dikili Tash Fig.33), in Mesopotamia since 4000BC (Tepe Gawra strainer flask, Fig. 65), and in the Indus valley since the 3rd millennium BC (Fig. 34).

While type a) evolved during the LMI A and B periods and published examples are known from Crete: Mochlos[92], Haghia Triada[93], Knossos[94], Kato Zakros[95], Palaikastro[96] (other specimens of different size have been found in the new excavations at Palaikastro "Chronique des fouilles en ligne, 2014 Fig.2: http://www.chronique.efa.gr/index.php/fiches/voir/4885/), and Gournià[97]. The variability of the size, including small and miniature specimens, found in palace environments, private houses, workshops and in the tomb outfits, suggests that they were employed for a small-scale production of luxuries as scented waters.

---

[92] Mochlos excavation of Richard Seager in 1908, reports many strainers from the houses of Block B, suggesting a specific employ of the inhabitants. A LM I strainer from western house of Block B. is published in Seager R.: 1908: American Journal Archaeology 13, 1909, 282, Pl. VII. S. Soles. Jeffrey "Mochlos" Expedition Magazine 20.2 (January 1978): Expedition Magazine. Penn Museum, January 1978 Web. 18 Aug 2017.
<http://www.penn.museum/sites/expedition/?p=4256>Soles J. S. & Davaras C. 1994: Excavations at Mochlos, in Hesperia 63-4, 391-435; and in Hesperia 1993: 61, 413-445.
[93] Footed strainer from the LM IB destruction horizon at Hagia Triada (Halbherr, Stefani & Banti 1977, fig. 11),
[94] Ν. Δημοπουλου- Ρεθεμιωτακη, *Το Αρχαιολογικό Μουσείο Ηρακλείου* (2005) 276.
[95] Platon 1974. p. 197, fig. 119. Hogarth 1900-1901, fig. 43; Hogarth 1902, pp. 335-338, tav. XII, 2; Dawkins 1903, p. 255, fig. 20.
[96] Bosanquet-Dawkins 1923, p. 77, fig. 61; p. 102, fig. 85a; p. 111, fig. 96a; Sackett, Popham 1970, p. 225, fig. 15.
[97] Boyd Hawes et alii, 1908, tav. VII, 21, IX, 1 (=Zervos 1956, p. 304, figs. 439, 441).

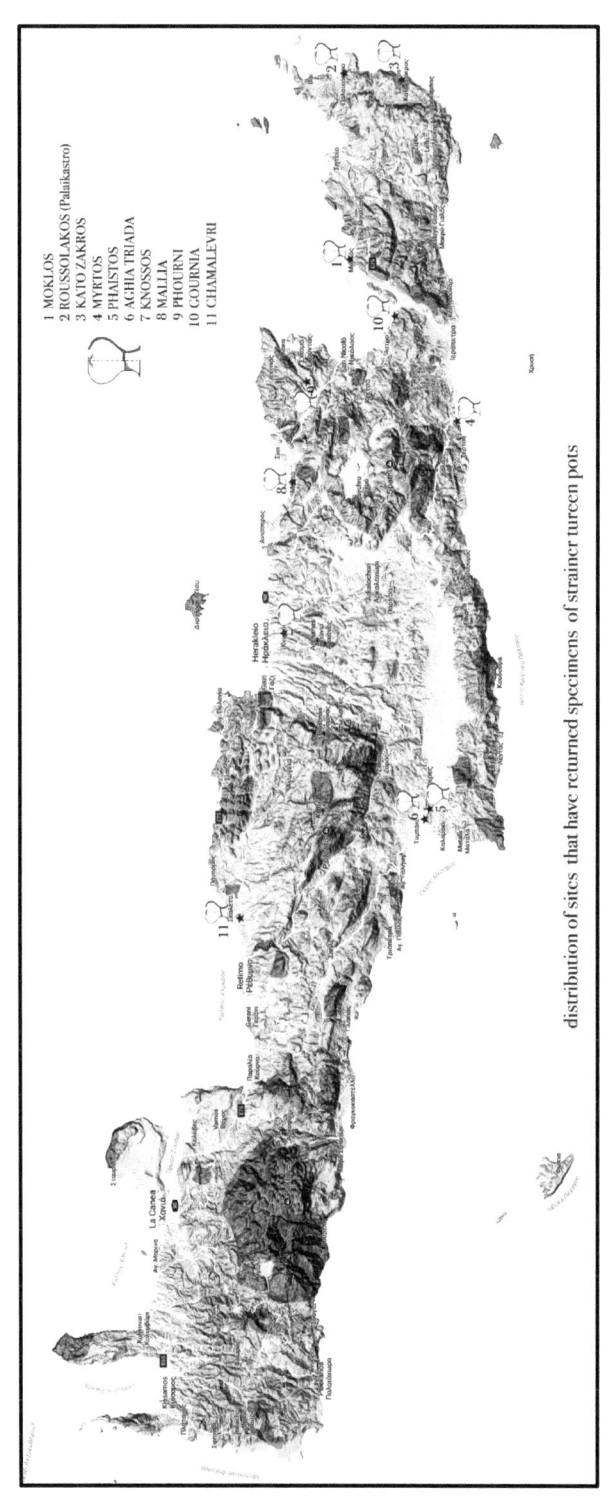

distribution of sites that have returned specimens of strainer tureen pots

Turning back to the most ancient examples from the Palace of Phaistos, decorated in Kamares style[98], we find a recent paper of Filippo Carinci[99], who published the excavations together with the director of the dig, Doro Levi in 1988[100]. It addresses the proposal of a new interpretation of the vases suggesting the preparation of ceremonial liquids (beverages) which thus implies filtering was an integral part of the ritual.

The scholar recognises three groups of strainers, of which only the first two (A and B) may be considered as part of specific apparatuses.

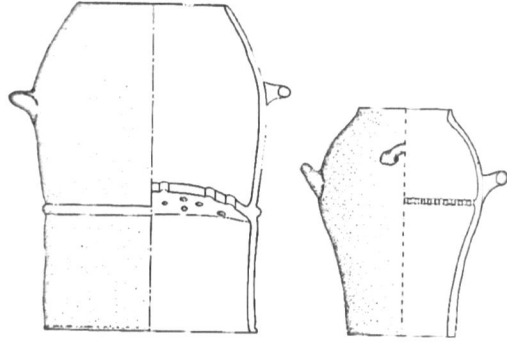

Fig. 87: Vases belonging to Carinci group A: n°1038 and n°14.

To the first group (A) belong two vases which differ in size and structural details. The largest coming from room LV (F. n°1038, h. 36.5cm, dm. 28cm; Carinci 2012, 106) has a cylindrical body, rounded at the top, converging towards the whole mouth (Fig. 87). It has two opposing loops in the belly expansion, while the underside is distinguished from an external ribbing, corresponding to the graft of the internal strainer

---

[98] Levi D.: 1976: *Festos e la Civiltà Minoica* 102, pl. 114 e, f, g.
[99] Carinci F. 2011: Strumentazioni per il Filtraggio nei Contesti di Apparato del Primo Palazzo di Festòs in *Kretes Minoidos. Tradizione e identità minoica tra produzione artigianale, pratiche cerimoniali e memoria del passato,* Studi offerti a V. La Rosa 103-116. Padova.
[100] Carinci 2011; Levi-Carinci 1988.

diaphragm[101]. The second is smaller with the rounded upper part, and the lower one formed by a cylinder shrinking to the base. Neither of the two resembles the standard form of the tureen on conical trunk base that will have a huge success and spread into the next periods (Fig. 88).

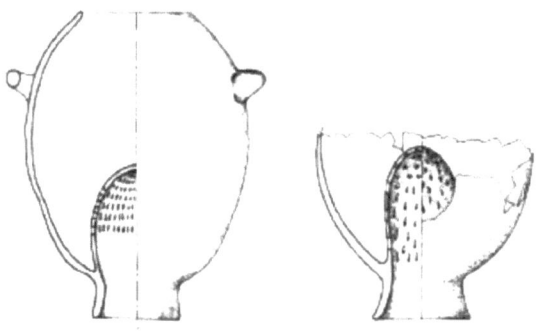

Fig. 88: Vases belonging to Carinci group B: n° 526 and n° 1595.

To the second group (B) belong two specimens almost identical in shape and size (n° 526: H. 40cm dm. 32cm; dm. foot 12,6cm; n° 1595 p. H. 22.6cm, dm. 30cm, dm. foot 13.5cm, characterized by an ovoid body with hole mouth and two opposite handles on a stumped open base, from which a strainer bulb rises. My attention was attracted by the fact that two specimens, one of group A, (F. 1038) and one of group B (F. 1595), have been found in the same place, room LV, 1,50 metres far from each other.

F. 1595 was in a very fragmentary condition, but in the lower part was preserved a fine painted decoration similar of the F.1038, suggesting the provenience from the same workshop, or a specific relation between them.

The description of the pottery distribution in room LV given by Carinci focuses on the close position of the strainers and in the presence as well as

---

[101] It recalls the Chinese steamer Tséng illustrated by Needham (1980, 27. Fig. 1473C), suggesting a careful looking in Festòs pottery repertoire to recognize the missing parts of the apparatuses.

of numerous tableware vases, and furniture, two tripods cooking pots and a storage jar 64cm high. He suggests that the two devices (F.1595 and F.1038) were in connexion with this jar and the filtering operation was made by people holding the vases from the handles on its top, as the diameter of mouth jar (33,35cm) was too large to support the objects.

My interpretation is quite different and involves one of the two tripod cooking pots found together in room LV, whose use in the place seems to be confirmed by a sort of furnace in a corner (Fig. 89).

Trying to bring together the set into a functional apparatus for distilling scented waters or alcoholic beverages, I found that the diameters of the mouths and the bases of the three vessels allowed a vertical assembly without altering the normal shape (i.e. upside down as suggested by Puglisi[102]) of the vessels indicated by the position of the handles.

Fig. 89: Tripod pot and specimens n°1595 and n°1038 from Phaistos room LV.

The result is a columnar apparatus for steam stream distillation, composed by a tripod cooking pot, a pot with bulbous strainer and a pot

---

[102] Puglisi D.: 2010 Dal vassoio tripodato al kernos: un set di ceramiche TMIA da Haghia Triada, in Creta Antica 11 45-129 (p. 79, fig. 32).

with diaphragmatic strainer, which is similar to modern components of copper column distillers (Fig. 91). In this sequence, the tripod on the fire contains water, the bulbous strainer acts as a container of organic substances and the pot with diaphragmatic strainer has the double function of filtering the steam and supporting the vase, where the liquid drops by an artifice closing the top.

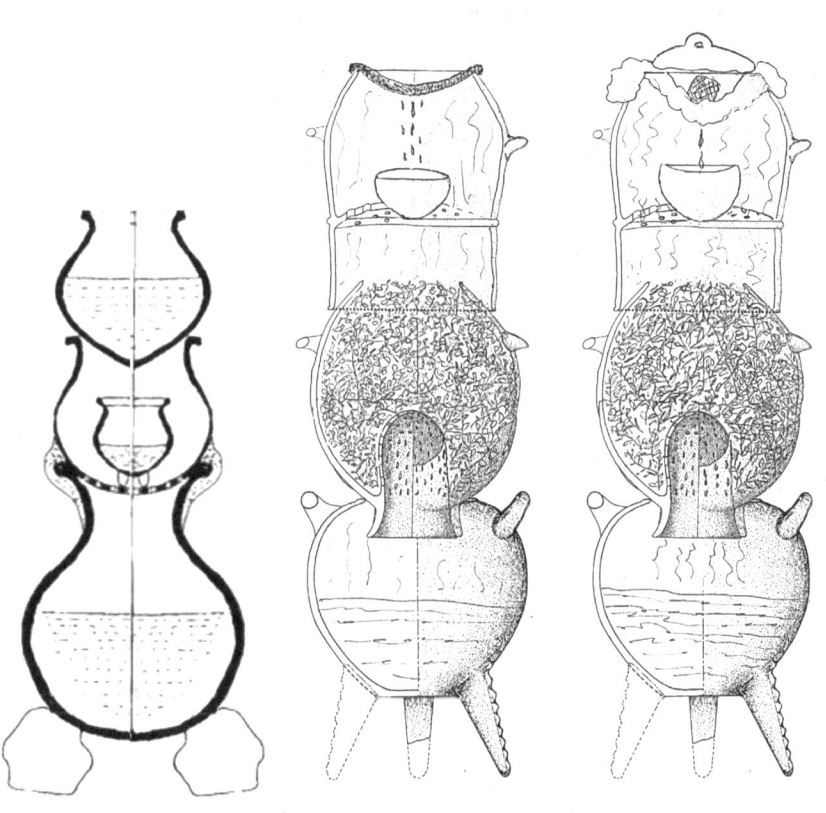

Fig. 90: a) Mahdihassan 1972 fig.2; b) Phaistos apparatus with a concave bottom pot as cover; c) Phaistos apparatus with a fleece as cover.

To close the top of the columnar apparatus, we have two different possibilities: first to put a pot with a concave bottom vase on the mouth (Fig. 90b), as in the Indian apparatus graphic restitution published by Mahdihassan (Fig. 90a), or second to close the top with a fleece of wool (or a cloth) bent inside with a stone (Fig. 90c), and blocked by a normal lid on the rim[103].

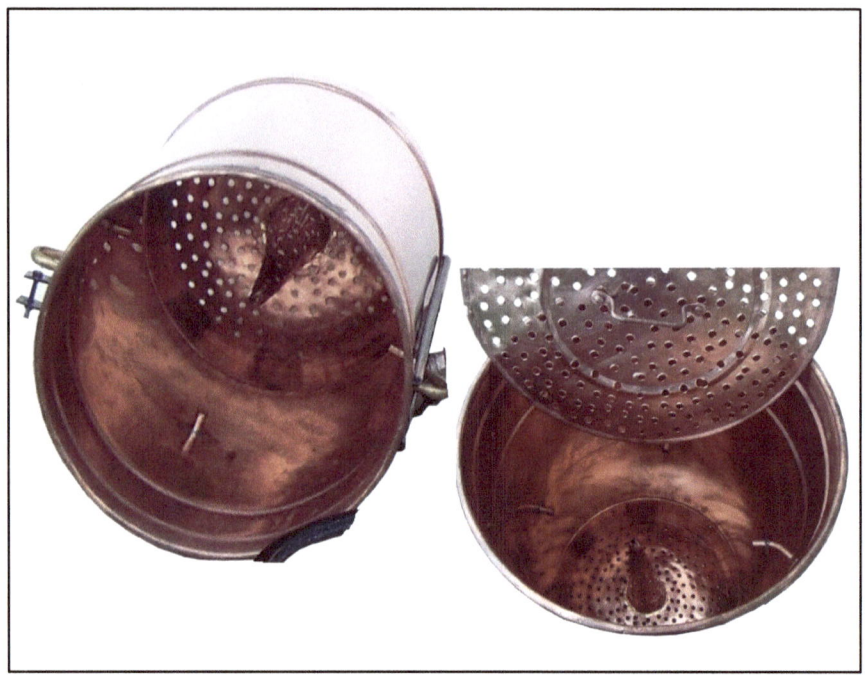

Fig. 91: Components of columnar distiller with a conical strainer bulb inside.

For the second possibility, I refer to Needham[104], and the linear B tablets from Knossos (KN Od 8202) and Pylos (PY Un 249) regarding the making of ointments, where wool appears together with ingredients allocated to an unguent boiler (Killen 1962b).

Among the different interpretations on these tablets, Shelmerdine (1985, 19) puts in direct relation the wool with the producing of fragrances affirming that: "finally the wool listed here was most probably used for

---

[103] Two of the strainers were found tapped with a lid, also decorated with pictorial motifs but not made by the same artisan, suggesting a casual employ of them: Marinatos, *Thera II*, pl. E. 2 and 10.
[104] Needham: 1980, p.81, Fig. 1454 *(a')* Collection of distillate in a fleece or ball of floss above the liquid to be distilled. and *(b')* Conjectural central drip of distillate from such a fleece.

straining the perfumed oil". The wool is thus assigned a specific function which is not far from the employment we suggest[105].

Wool reminds us of a famous passage of Plato in the "Symposium"[106], and considering the hydro repellence of the fibres, a cloth of wool is perfect as a condenser [107]for hydrosol, while retaining essential oils in its fibres, from which it is possible to recover by squeezing the fleece at the end of the processing.

A fragment of vegetable textiles found at Thera, together with one of these devices suggests the employ of simple cloths[108].

---

[105] Françoise Rougemont 2014: Sheep Rearing Wool Production and Management in Mycenaean Written Documents in C. Breniquet, C. Michel ed. Wool Economy in the Ancient Near East, 340-371. Pliny also describes method of condensing turpentine vapour on fleeces of wool hung over the pot containing the heated material; this is the same method as that used by the sailors at sen.* Pliny, lib. XV, cl). 7.

-Ann Harman 2015: "One very old description is of a crude distillation that involved a pot of water filled with cedar and water with lamb's wool stretched over the top to catch the rising vapours. The wool was periodically wrung out and collected resulting in an early distillate water".

[106] "Socrates then sitting down, observed, 'It would be well, Agatho, if wisdom were a thing of such a kind as to flow from the party filled with it to the one who is less so, when they touch each other, like water in vessels running by means of a thread of wool from the fuller vessel into the emptier". Plato's works, Burges's translation, vol. III., p. 480 (Bohn).

[107] "The cells of wool fibres have a waxy coating, making wool water repellent, but still allowing absorption of water vapour. The water-repellent surface makes wool garments naturally shower-proof and also reduces staining because spills don't soak in easily".

108- Platon 1974. p. 197, fig. 119. Specimens from house A e I, cfr. Hogarth 1900-1901, fig. 43; Hogarth 1902, pp. 335-338, tav. XII, 2; Dawkins 1903, p. 255, fig. 20; Marinatos 1999A, pp. 13, 23, 27 e fig. 18, tav. E, 2, 8, tav. 10,1; Marinatos 1999A, p. 53, tav. A, 1, tav. 48, 2; Marinatos 1999 C, p. 19, tav. 27b; Marinatos 1999 D, 33, tavv. 73b, 78a.

Marinatos S. *Excavations at Thera II (1968 season)* (1969), pl. E. 2 and 10; Marinatos S., *Excavations at Thera VI (1972 season)* (1974). *Thera VI*, pl. 78a. Kriga D. 2014: Flora and Fauna Iconography on Strainers and Kymbai at Akrotiri: Theran Ceramic Vessels of Special Use and Special Iconography *499-505*, in Aegaeum 37: *Actes de la 14e Rencontre égéenne internationale, Paris, Institut National d'Histoire de l'Art (INHA)*11-14 décembre 2012.

More examples of the tureen type from the Aegean islands[109], Keos[110] and Melos[111], testify how long the type circulated.

Though the evolution and employ of this device has been a subject of discussion and different interpretations for almost a century, I would like to add my personal observation not regarding the chronological evolution of the shape from the cylindrical/oval type (Phaistos Fig. 87 and Thera, oval specimen of Fig. 92) to the rounded tureen (Fig. 85) and its distribution in the Mediterranean during the Mycenaean period, but on the possible dissemination of the technological knowledge achieved as a cultural suggestion for shaping new still apparatuses.

♍

The Tureen shape which had the massive diffusion until the end of the Late Bronze age is a very simple device, which we find still today in copper versions as component of many steam stream distillers. Otherwise, it may have inspired the shape of the dome alembic, having in common the rounded head working as the expansion vase and the conical base working as a flange to set the alembic on the boiler.

Of course, when the device became a closed pot the spout assumed the function of recovering the condensed liquid, but the shape remained almost the same, preserving its main functional elements. It is curious to note that in the clay and copper models even the handles of the Minoan/Mycenaean pattern have been sometimes conserved.

---

[109] Edgar C.C.1904: Phylakopi (Melos) in Atkinson et al. 128, Pl. XXIV.
[110] Georgiou H.S. 1986, Keos VI, Ayia Irini. Specialized and Industrial Pottery, 43, nn. 173-176, tavv.12, 21. Mainz.
[111] Smith C. and Welch F.B. *Excavations at Phylakopi in Melos- conducted by the British School at Athens* (1904).

Fig. 92: Three different size of the tureen shaped strainers from Santorini Thera, in comparison with a modern copper strainer "component" of a commercial alembic.

However, it's out of the question that the columnar apparatus composed of three elements, including the strainer (in some cases two), is still one of the most widely used apparatus for producing aromatic waters in the Levant and North African countries (Fig. 93). As in the Phaistos hypothesis, the first cylinder holds water, the second flowers, while the third collects the condensation of the steam stream, dropping outside through a taped pipe.

Fig.93: Modern columnar copper apparatus for distillation of perfumed water, commonly used in Morocco (high 160cm), including strainer components.

XII. Egypt

Fig. 94: Position of Kerma in ancient Kush region.

In Egypt, since the Pre-dynastic period, the situation is very different from Mesopotamia and Aegean, because until today we do not have clear descriptions of distillation technology in hieroglyphic texts, as we find in the cuneiform tablets of the Akkadian period. Despite the incredible legacy of cosmetic and pharmaceutical recipes Egypt left in the world, it was never found a workshop or an alchemical laboratory connected to a religious environment. Only from the Egyptian tombs we have informed of the existence of them, because most of the outfits contain since the Predynastic period objects and ointments for the care of the body.

As this civilization is the only one to have returned a huge repertoire of recipes, most of which are still valid, any missing evidence for a working place is an unprecedented reality that takes our attention.

I would like to emphasize the findings in the Neolithic tombs of Naqada I, II and III (IV millennium BC) of objects of personal beauty as palettes, pestles, and ointments because they are an important social evolution in human history. These tombs do not belong to special élite people, furthermore we find remedies among the funeral goods.

This material testifies that something extraordinary was happening. It was something that would change the story of science and technology, giving birth to the medical science in Egypt. Everything started around 4200 BC at the end of the Badarian period with a few unshaped palettes and small stone containers, bottles and boxes for ointments going hand in hand with the emergence of the great Nilotic civilization.

The constant evolution that accompanies the first millennium of the Egyptian culture until the early dynasties is a period in which the cornerstone of technology and science was expressed in 360 degrees in all arenas of human knowledge, from medicine to architecture; from writing to religious beliefs.

This chronological interchange seems to find an explanation for the discovery of the 700 wine-jars found in the grave of King Scorpion in 1990.

The tomb was built around 3150 BC (Naqada III A2 period) and the vessels containing spiced wine coming from different sites of Southern Palestine. Analyses carried out on the clay of the stoppers that sealed the jars indicated that they were Egyptian, as the spices are also like to be.

This observation opened several discussions on the taste, use and adding of spices (coming from the Egyptian environment) to the wine included in the funeral equipment of King Scorpion[112] according and to a herbal knowledge already widespread and practiced.

But some wine was produced also in Egypt since seeds of grapes have been found in Predynastic (4000-3050 BC) settlements of Tell El-Farain (Buto) and Tell Ibrahim Awad, located in the Nile Delta.[113] This detail has some importance, as in this period some spouted vases start to appear in the clay repertoire of Predynastic and Protodynastic Egypt.

From the tomb of King Djoser (III dynasty, Old Kingdom around 2600 BC), we have the first written document that affirms the king's wine came from "the vineyard of the red house of the king's house in the town of *Senpu* in the western *nomes*", confirming that in Egypt the history of wine follows in parallel to that of pharmaceutical compounds and cosmetics[114].

The distinction that the Egyptians had among the different types of wine, identifying notes through the smell and taste, makes us realize how much they were experts on it as well as its employment.

In fact, the prescriptions often recommend the use of *old wine*, suggesting that the Egyptians knew that the aging wine takes on a different alcohol content, increasing year-by-year, turning it into a versatile

---

[112] B. Handwerk 2009. Scorpion King's Wines Egypt's Oldest, Spiked with Meds, in *National Geographic News* April 13. McGovern, Patrick E., Ulrich Hartung, Virginia R. Badler, Donald L. Glusker, and Lawrence J. Exner 1997 The Beginnings of Winemaking and Viniculture in the Ancient Near East and Egypt. Expedition 39(1):3–21

7 Zohary D, Hopf M. Domestication of Plants in the Old World: The Origin and Spread of Cultivated Plants in West Asia, Europe, and the Nile Valley. Oxford: Oxford Univ Press; 2000. Pp. 205–206; Murray, Mary Anne, 2000. Viticulture and wine production, in: Ancient Egyptian Materials and Technology. (eds. P. Nicholson and I. Shaw). Cambridge University Press, 577-608.

[114] P.E. Mc Govern, A. Mirzoian, G. R. Hall, 2009: Ancient Egyptian herbal wines, Proc Natl Acad Sci U S A. May 5; 106(18): 7361–7366. Published online 2009 Apr 13. Doi: 10. 1073/ pnas.0811578106.

substance that can react better in alchemical compositions. The famous medical papyri report many pharmaceutical recipes include wine as the main ingredient from which to start preparing the potion. This massive presence and use of wine, which will become one of the favourite elements in future distillation, makes it difficult to imagine that a person, so careful in use and research of the most precious substances in making remedies for every type of illness, did not notice the natural vaporization and condensation process that took place during the preparation of these recipes. However, what is missing in the papyruses is any description of the equipment and instruments to prepare them. The absence of any report about the essential paraphernalia required and the lack of any archaeological discovery of places recognisable as laboratories contrasts with the word Alchemy, the meaning of which goes back to Egypt. In fact, since the era of the Pharaohs, Egypt was called Kemet by Keme-Kimy = black soil. And according to an accredited theory from this name derives the Arabic word "al-Kemy", which simply means "science of Egypt". We could consider this a legendary etymological derivation if the history of Alchemy did not recognize in an Egyptian its most ancient and influential representative.

A character so important that even the Catholic Church recognized its scientific and philosophical prestige (Fig. 95), albeit few scholars accept Hermes Trismegistus, author of many lost treaties and of the famous alchemical fragment known as Emerald Tablet[115] (discovered amidst the

---

[115] The Emerald Tablet, *teaching the unity of matter and the basic*, in conjunction with the works of the Jabir, *The Sum of the Perfect Magistery*, *The Investigation of Perfection,* and his *Testament* is still considered what arrived us of the Egyptian sacred art of alchemy. There have been various stories of the origin of the tract, one being that the original emerald slab upon which the precepts were said to be inscribed in Phoenician characters was discovered in the tomb of Hermes by Alexander the Great, as report the Berne edition of 1545 of Jabir Summa perfectionis (under the name of The Emeralds

writings of Jabir, alias, Abou Moussah Djfar-Al Sell 750 AD), really existed.

Fig. 95: Hermes, Mercurius, Trismegistus, floor mosaic at the entrance of Siena Cathedral, by Giovanni di Stefano 1488, Italy
https://commons.wikimedia.org/w/index.php?curid=761099.

But if we can consider legendary the figure of Hermes Trismegistus, supposedly born around the 1900 BC, his writings were considered the Bible of alchemical science, we cannot pass silently the name and works

---

Tables of Hermes the Thrice Great Concerning Chemistry…..*words written on The Tablet of Emerald found between his hands in a dark cave wherein his body was discovered buried*").

of a great Egyptian physician born nearly a thousand years before Trismegistus, whom we have ample testimony.[116]

Imhotep, the Vizier and Physician of King Zoser born at Menfi in 2680 BC and died in 2600, really existed. His life and renowned arts are described in many Egyptian texts, and part of his medical prescriptions are recorded in the famous *papyrus of Smith* which report 48 clinical cases. Architect, poet, and scientist doctor, he also covered the office of Kheriheb her-tep (first priest). Then, thanks to his fame and merit acquired in life, he entered the Egyptian Pantheon of the minor gods, wearing his amulet then became a defence and remedy for many illnesses.

We are in the 3rd millennium BC under the kingdom of Sekhemkhet Zoser of the 3rd Egyptian Dynasty, when medicine, and surgical science (not to mention the architecture and metallurgy) had already reached levels comparable to those of Europe at the end of the Modern Era. But no representation or model of an Egyptian pharmaceutical workshop of the time has been left by the scholars and physicians, as if everything happened in the absolute secret, perhaps to let people believe of a secret or magical ingredient. However, a new pot appears at the beginning of the 2nd millennium BC, in the near Kingdom of Kush, in the Kerma region (Fig. 94), high Nubia and actual North Sudan among the Black Topped ware repertoire that inherited shapes and colours from the previous Egyptian Naqada and Badarian culture of the 4th/3rd millennium BC. In this very fine ware, among the traditional shapes, with straight or flaring walls and hole mouth, we find a spouted type, whose excellent quality and elegance enhanced by the extremely thin and long spout suggest an intriguing use (Fig. 96). The comparison with the

---

[116] Jamieson Boyd Hurry, *Imhotep, the Vizier and Physician of King Zoser and Afterwards the Egyptian God of Medicine* London, Oxford University Press, 1926.

preceding spouted jars or jug of Kerma and Egyptian repertoires, underlines the difference, for the complete absence of any grip, and the magisterial craftsmanship to make by hand egg shell extruded walls and an extremely thin and long spout that not having craftsmanship background required a special commitment.

It's just the detail of the spout out of measure that makes difficult to include the pot in *the Kerma typological horizon* for personal or domestic use, as the possibility to give a specific use to this vase are few. The Nubian repertoire, better known as *Kerma pottery ware* has a very characteristic typological horizon, including bowls, beakers, and jars among which this spouted pot makes a strong difference[117].

Fig. 96: Kerma spouted bowl. Courtesy British Museum London.

---

[117] Except in case it was invented for a specific use, which I suggest was distillation.

Besides, the quality of the ware texture and the treatment of the surfaces inside and outside is so high and fine that it is hard to find a comparison.

We can only see that we cannot use the spout to suck the liquid inside, as its position on the upper body is too high. Obviously, the comparison with the standard form of glass alembic head (Fig. 45) is immediate to the eye, and becomes even more consistent if we examine separately the individual elements that make up the pot, comparing them with a Medieval still head.

The striking resemblance is based not only on the dimensions (around 15x 20cm not considering the length of the spout) and the weight (around 250gr), but on the shape of the body, and the flaring neck which works as flange on the lower pot (cucurbita).

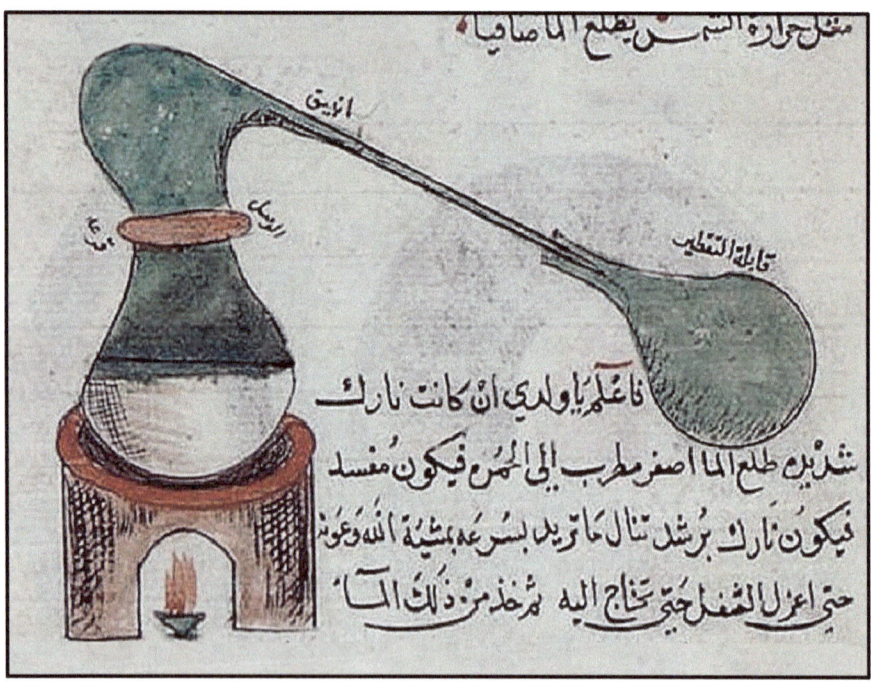

Fig. 97: Distillation by still treatise on Arabic alchemy, Middle East, 18th century. British Library of London Add. 25724, f.3

For comparison, I choose the famous illustration on a Jabir manuscript (Fig. 97), as it is considered one of the first medieval documentation of a glass alembic. It was an alembic head in the exhibition of the Archaeological Museum of Nicosia (Fig. 98) in Cyprus, which seems the direct copy of the Kerma's spouted bowl, despite the difference of more than 2800 years.

It is superfluous to argue about the more or less accentuated shape of the neck, the length of the spout, and the presence or absence of the inner channel, as we have testimonies of countless versions of glass and copper in which these elements are accentuated or even absent. Any scholar who has been involved in distillation knows that with these pots you can distil perfectly.

Fig. 98: Comparison between two specimens of Kerma spouted bowl and a Medieval glass alembic from Cyprus (in the middle), Archaeological Museum, Nicosia.

So, we do not need proof from experimental archaeology to demonstrate the functionality of these vases, and among the Kerma repertoire we can find a number of common jars which we can use as a cucurbita to assemble an apparatus.

What happened in Egypt in the span of years that separate the Kerma spouted pot from the first alembic heads of the Late Roman period is unknown. But, undoubtedly the specimens conserved in the Cairo Museum and in many European museums, including the Archaeological

Museum of Naples, the Louvre at Paris, and the British Museum in London, are very similar in the limits of a blown-glass object created in an environment completely different from a ceramist laboratory, which nevertheless seems to follow the standardized pattern of 2000 BC Kerma.

Among the many unsolved mysteries about the origin of the extraordinary Egyptian Science, which anticipated tens of centuries other contemporary civilization, we should probably include the invention of the dome still head.

An invention which had a success entirely different from that of the Mesopotamian steamer that was never replicated in glass or metal. What makes the pot more interesting for me is that it belongs to the class of Black Topped ware which has parallels in the Red Polished Black-Topped that appears in the same period in Cyprus. This is a circumstance that I will use after to speculate on the Egyptian provenance of the Pyrgos alembic heads.

Fig. 99: Kerma spouted bowl, Nubia Museum Aswan.

The correct functionality of the Kerma spouted bowl is attested by the fact that, over the centuries, the object has been replicated without real changes, in different materials (clay, glass, and metal), entering de facto in every chemical workshop and pharmaceutical industry.

Unluckily, few specimens survived the rich outfits of the alchemical laboratories depicted in the paintings of time, thanks the fragility of glass and the possibility to melt the broken fragments to make new ones.

Despite this, the pictures representing alchemical laboratories of 1600 and later, conserved an image of the shape during the centuries (Fig.100).

Fig 100: David Teniers the Younger: Koninkliik Museum Schone Kunsten (Anvers)

The copper specimen had a different evolution and shape interpretation according to the use and countries, entering into the industry of alcohol production and liquors, each having a longer life because of the metal.

Moreover, clay still contrivances with the onion head are attested in Europe, Near and Middle East, Pakistan, and India from the beginning of the medieval period with many specimens and fragments are preserved in the museums. Looking at them we realise how they are like the Egyptian prototypes. Some of them have been used to distil metals and chemical substances, some for pharmaceutical compounds and others for hydrosols and essential oils. Although few of them have been properly analysed.

Anyhow, still today many ceramic workshops in Italy sell clay alembic equipment, with a simple dome head, without any collar to keep the condensation inside, for home distilling essences.

XIII. Pyrgos/Mavroraki Cyprus

Cyprus is an island whose cultural heritage is less known to the vast public than Mesopotamia, Crete, and Egypt from which the most ancient writing, architecture, philosophy and religion come. However, its extraordinary location in the Eastern corner of the Mediterranean, facing the Aegean islands, and embraced by Anatolia and Near Eastern civilization sealed its fate through the millennia making the island one of most suitable places to trade luxuries (Fig. 101).

Fig. 101: Cyprus location in the Eastern corner of the Mediterranean.

During the Neolithic period, Cyprus gradually became a crucial exchanging point in Eastern Mediterranean trade, and its civilization appears from the start as part of a large cultural subsystem related to foreign suggestions.

In the Early Bronze age, the intensive production of perfumes, as witnessed by the large number of clay perfume bottles, like Egyptian' alabasters, suggests that the import and export of spices, resins and fragrances was still one of the most important trade and economic supply.

Obviously, the environmental resources greatly influenced the production of aromatic waters and essential oils, which used the Mediterranean flora and wild olive trees that Cyprus was very rich in (Fig. 102). The island still today owns a botanical heritage of great interest which includes oily, aromatic, and pharmaceutical species.

Fig. 102: Cyprus inland forest rich of Mediterranean flora.

At the end of the third millennium BC, Cyprus diverged radically from Egypt and from the schemes of other contemporary Mediterranean cultures, first for the absence of a status difference among the people (as the outfits of the tombs attest), and secondly because they had started to exploit the rich mineral and botanical resources of the island. This was by far the most important period connected to the evolution of a prestige merchandise; the Mediterranean Bronze Age is marked to significant exchanges among emerging civilizations and elites. In Cyprus, there are highlights aspects of an industrial revolution which brought within the market quality Cypriot products, deeply changing the model of life, the extension of the settlements and shape of houses. The small village (only of one or two hectares as Tepe Gawra) enlarged to 30 hectares, the house lost its circular plant becoming rectangular and the tombs were located outside the inhabited area.

Fig. 103: Map of Cyprus with the position of Pyrgos/Mavroraki site.

The position of some villages is so well select that many modern correspond to the sites of the Bronze age, demonstrating the uninterrupted occupation of well-chosen places to inhabit, thanks the proximity of natural resources, minerals, and water. In the same period, in Anatolia, the Aegean Sea and upper Egypt people were reworking the technological

Mesopotamians suggestions drove through the caravan traffics, inventing instrumental pots different of type and similar in technology.

It is no wonder, then that we find Cyprus, already at the beginning of the 2nd millennium BC, with technologies able to produce products through distillation such as essential oils and aromatic waters. Pyrgos is located on the Southern coast in Limassol district, one of the six districts in which the island was divided before 1974 (Fig. 103). The picture of the Bronze Age Pyrgos is like most of the Eastern Mediterranean villages: a long line of houses constructed with mud bricks on stone foundations bordering the sides of a seasonal stream[118].

Fig. 104: Aerial view of Pyrgos village with the indication of Mavroraki.

---

[118] Belgiorno 2016 and 2017 a;

The houses were roughly rectangular, some with an open court, generally of one storey; the roof was constructed with wooden beams and mats of reeds, sealed with a thick layer of mud. The place was often utilized for domestic purposes, including to dry fruits and vegetables, and it was accessible via a wooden stair positioned inside the house in a corner corresponding an opening in the ceiling (Fig. 105). Other wooden beams were used for doors, windows, and outdoor sheds, under which, large stone mills, and mortars were often placed. Few streets run across the village as most houses were leaning against each other.

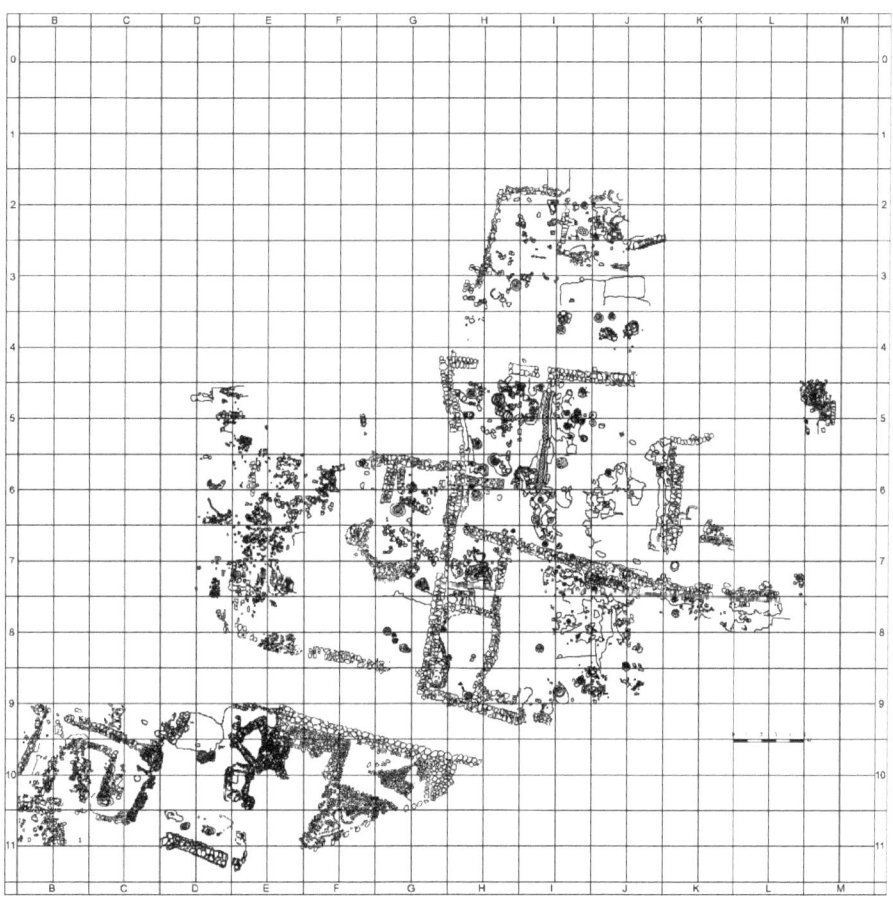

Fig. 105: Map of Pyrgos/Mavroraki excavations

The surrounding environment was quite different from today, because the climate was more humid and green fields, forest, ponds, and several smaller streams surrounded the village as today. The industrial complex, probably a unitary building like an oriental modern souk, was in the middle of the settlement, but unfortunately today it is mostly occupied by modern houses and villas (Fig. 104).

The extension of the industrial market is difficult to calculate as the southern side is cut by the old road connecting Pyrgos to Pareklisha.

Instead, the north side seems to go up to the Mavroraki hill where small soundings in 2011 and 2012 confirmed the presence of more workshops.

This evidence suggests that it occupied an area, of three hectares or more, which indicate Pyrgos had some importance as a centre of production and trade in the first half of the II millennium BC.

Fig. 106: 3D reconstruction of the main building of Pyrgos, by Simone Jacomini.

The intact context of Pyrgos dating back to the abandonment of the site in the Middle Bronze age, probably from an earthquake, gives us a rare possibility of comparison with late laboratories and market places.

It seems that the community was addressed to specific productions that did not need a monumental structure to run, but large spaces organised, unitary in nature, arranged individual working places for different activities (Fig. 106). In some of them, the coexistence of metallurgy with cosmetic/medical production provokes thoughts of comparison with the medieval alchemical laboratory often represented and described in the alchemical books as places where both the activities were performed[119].

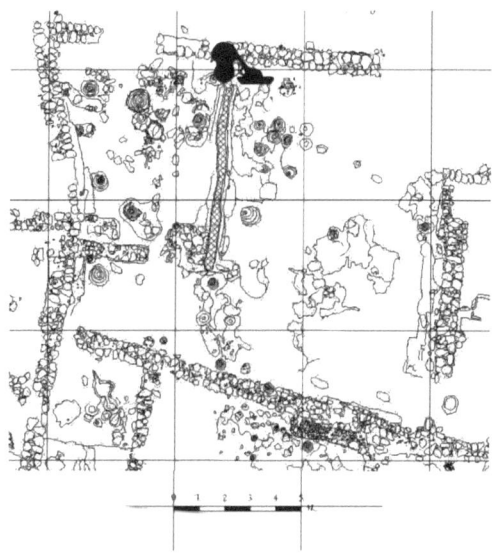

Fig. 107: Pyrgos olive mill and perfumery ground map.

---

119 If we compare the material of the alchemical laboratory found in 1980 at Kirchberg am Wagram in Austrian Oberstockstall we can identify the Pyrgos industrial complex as a proto alchemical community area: Sigrid von Osten, "Das Alchemistenlaboratorium Oberstockstall. Ein Fundcomplex des 16. Jahrhunderts aus Niederosterreich" PhD dissertation Universitata Wien 1992; Rudolf Werner Soukup and Helmut Mayer, Alchemistisches . Martelli M. 2011: Greek Alchemists at Work: 'Alchemical Laboratory' in the Greco-Roman Egypt, Nuncius 26, 271–311. Martinon-Torres M. 2012: The Archaeology of Alchemy and Chemistry in the Early Modern World: An Afterthought in Archaeology International No. 15, 2011-2012, 33-36.

The workshops enjoyed many facilities, including water and an unlimited availability of stone tools made from local flint and basalt bedrock, where the architectural structures rest. Extensive agriculture, animal gathering, transporting and provision of organic and inorganic material from land and sea were probably the main engagements of the people not directly involved in the production.

The index of the cooperative system from which the unitary complex evolved is given by the presence of a large central room mainly occupied by a monumental olive press (Fig. 109), which divided the place into two connected spaces, for storage and production (Fig. 107). The room measures 15 metres by 18, it was the fulcrum of the industrial complex, communicating on three sides with other workshops involved in the production of textiles and copper objects.

Fig. 108: The oil mill of Pyrgos, with the central pole bench, the storage room on the right and the perfumery area on the left.

The place had probably different busy periods during the year, presuming that the olive press was working only for three or four months, and the rest of the year was mainly involved in the production of perfumes and cosmetic pharmacological compounds (Fig. 108), as the Archaeometry investigations suggest[120].

Furnaces with pits for maceration still containing the jugs, funnels, and fragments of hundreds of ceramics, crushed beneath the collapsed walls, were the first evidence of a possible earthquake that destroyed the site, forcing the people to abandon their work in progress. Archaeometry investigations confirmed the hypothesis, adding more details to the scenario and the destination of the hundreds of ceramics in fragments, mortars, querns and of stone tools.

Fig. 109: 3D reconstruction of the *oil mill of Pyrgos, with the press working with a pole.*

The presence of carbons in pit furnaces, and the fact that some fragments of vases crushed in the collapse were black due to long periods of time exposed to fire (in the reduction of oxygen), confirmed that the furnaces at the time of the disaster were still lit, place in full swing (Fig. 110).

---

[120] Lentini 2007, 2009, 2017.

In a space arranged at the end of the bench holding the beam of the press (Fig. 112), dividing the storage area of the press room of the East wing set up to produce perfumes and cosmetics, we found under the collapsing of the north wall the remains of a double furnace with fragments of large pots and basins scattered for two meters (Fig. 110 and Fig. 111). It took two years of restoration and Archaeometry analysis[121] to make sense of what had emerged in that space.

Fig. 110 (and Fig.111): Fragmentary remains of the still apparatus distributed for 2m: the furnace (on the right), the large basin on the left, the alembic head in the middle with the spout visible in foreground, and some fragments burn inside the kiln together with a jar.

The fragments belonged to two large jugs, two huge basins, two large spouted pots (all Red Polished metallic ware), and two cooking pots

---

[121] Archaeometry, Palynological and Botanical investigations on the organic remains, plants and seeds from the excavation of Pyrgos/Mavroraki have been coordinated by A. Lentini in the laboratory of ITABC-CNR Rome, where the samples are conserved. Lentini Scala 2004, 2006; Lentini Belgiorno 2008.

(coarse ware). The fragment distribution revealed that some vessels were connected to each other, in particular the large basin housed one of the jugs that had fallen in the direction of the larger spout vessel, which in turn was found along with another vessel around the furnace.

Fig. 111: The jug on the left of the basin with the neck turning in the direction of the basin and alembic head.

All pots have been completely restored with the exception of a coarse ware cooking pot. At the time of the disaster, the fire was lit as you can see from the blackened fragments of the restored pots. The assembling of the pots gave two sets for distillation each composed of four pieces (one missing the lower part), one of which was probably working[122], as the fragments found inside the furnace suggest.

---

[122] Belgiorno 2016 chapter 6.

Around the heap of the fragments there were four large basalt querns (Fig. 112), many pestles, and many flints, meanwhile the double pit furnace coated with stone pebbles was against the stone foundations of the wall. All the ceramics belonging to the sets were made completely by hand without the use of the lathe, and quality fired at high temperatures[123].

Fig. 112: The restored two alembic heads and large basins brought back in situ with the querns found nearby.

The apparatus found in connection with the furnace is composed of a large basin (dm. 55cm Fig. 113) holding a jug (H. 50 cm) and a jar (H. 49cm) holding a domed pot (H. 49cm, Fig. 117), with three handles and a long spout entering perfectly into the neck of the jug.

The spouted pot and the basin are decorated with the same incised and applied decorations suggesting they were made by the same artisan, or

---

[123] Belgiorno 2016, chapter 6.

indicating they belonged to a specific set. The most important consists of 4 rings of fake rope applied at a calculate distance around the spout.

The same decoration of fake rope is under the base of the large basin (Fig. 113) in an unusual position for a decoration, unless it is a sign of recognition, or a stabilizing.

The spouted pot appears in Cyprus in the Early Bronze age and it is present in different sizes and shapes in all the bronze age repertoire.

But this version seems the sum of structural (and technological) suggestions coming from the Aegean tureen pot for the shape (Fig. 92) of the neck and the handles, from the Anatolian fake teapots (Fig. 74) for the domed body, and from Kerma Egypt spouted bowl (Fig.99) for the flaring neck and inclination of the spout[124].

In any case, it is very likely that the "fake" rope rings refers to some previous negative experiences, when a real rope was added in emergency around smoothed spouts to seal a piece of cloth or skin or something else to better joint the spout and the neck of the jug, and under the basin to avoid its moving.

In addition, the large basin (Fig. 113), provided with four wide perforated grips, reports two small ideograms engraved after the firing of the vessel, one composing of three lines, the second of five (Fig. 121). They have been intentionally made in an asymmetrical manner on the rim of one handle.

---

[124] The finding may seem extraordinary for the time and the place, but if we consider devices for distil the Hittite fake teapots of Hattusa and the spouted bowls of Kerma both dating back around the 1800 BC as the complex of Pyrgos, we should not be surprised to find similar specimens in the island that at the time had intense trades with Egypt and Anatolia, as the finding of Cypriot pottery on the Anatolian coast and until the fourth cataract of the Nile suggest.

The experiments made with a replica of Pyrgos' set have demonstrated that it was possible to use the device to produce hydrosol, essential oils, or spirits.[125]

Fig. 113: A student of Palazzo Spinelli of Florence restoring the large basin of the set. Well visible are the fragments burned by the firing carbons crashed and scattered together with the vases.

During the opening of the exhibitions organised at Trevi (Pg) in 2006, at Florence in 2008, at Viterbo in 2009[126] and Cyprus in 2010, replicas of the

---

[125] A. Bartoli & C. Cappelletti 2007. Antiquitates: Tecniche di archeologia sperimentale applicate alla riproduzione dei profumi, in M.R. Belgiorno, (a cura di) *I Profumi di Afrodite e il segreto dell'Olio*, Gangemi, Roma, 137-145.

[126] A. Bartoli, M.R. Belgiorno, C. Cappelletti and A. Lentini 2009. *Cipro: Un Sito di 4000 Anni fa e l'Archeologia Sperimentale*, Collana I Quaderni di Antiquitates, ed. Tuscia, Viterbo.

Fig. 114: Manjpur India: clay, modern set for distillation composed with the same four elements of Pyrgos, arranged on a mud-brick furnace.

Fig. 115: The alembic set of Pyrgos arranged according the fragments distribution in the exhibition at the Ethnographic Museum of Lefkara, Cyprus in 2010.

Pyrgos alembic worked for hours and produced hydrosol and essential oils of different plants.

The proves made with the replicas revealed interesting details suggesting that the success of distillation depends on many factors and escamotages.

As we can see in the 1600' pictures representing alchemical laboratories, the large alembics are on benches, stands, or built supports to control the fire that should never be in direct contact with the pot, reminding that different material needs different temperatures (Fig.126).

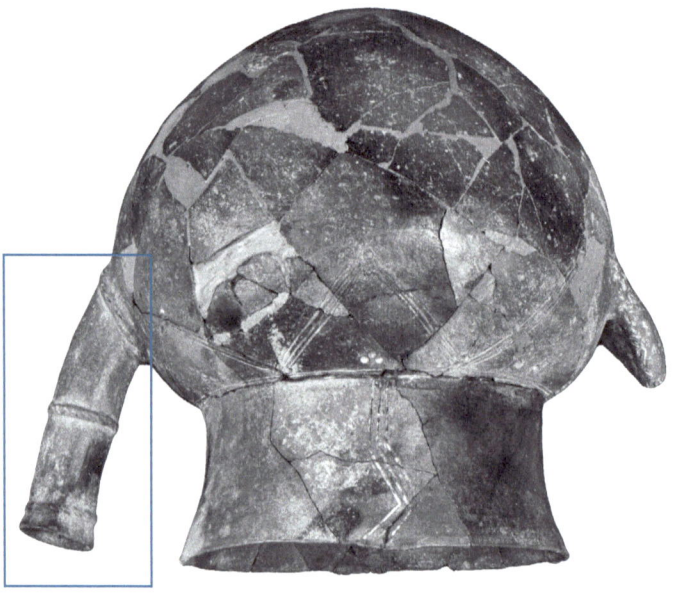

Fig. 116: Pyrgos Alembic head inv. N° 106, Limassol district Museum.
In the rectangle, the detail of the rings in relief around the spout.

The two sets of Pyrgos, which when assembled measure one meter and half each (Fig.115), were probably positioned on a feature made of crude mud bricks raising from the ground, on the double furnaces, which after the collapsing of the room melt with the mudbrick of the wall creating a packed stratum, which sealed the fragments of the two devices burning the fragments with the firing carbons. In assembling the four pieces of Pyrgos' set for distillation we found many contemporary rural comparisons, especially in India (Fig. 114). Another interesting observation coming from the experiments, gave a justification of the fake rope rings positioned at regular distances on both the spouts. We found that they are not a simple decoration, but have a specific function regarding the escaping of the steam during the distillation process (Fig. 116, Fig. 117 and modern comparison Fig. 118).

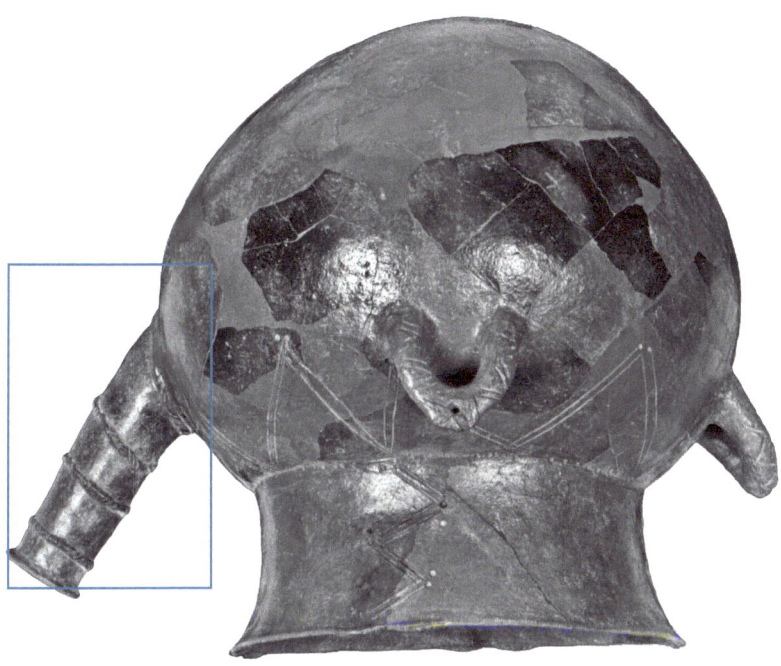

Fig. 117: Pyrgos Alembic head inv. N° 123, Limassol district Museum.
In the rectangle, the detail of the rings in relief around the spout.

The diameter of the neck of collectors may have different sizes for which you can fit the spout until you reach the correct ring. This also allows a better joining, rolling around a piece of cloth or skin with mud avoiding every loss of steam.

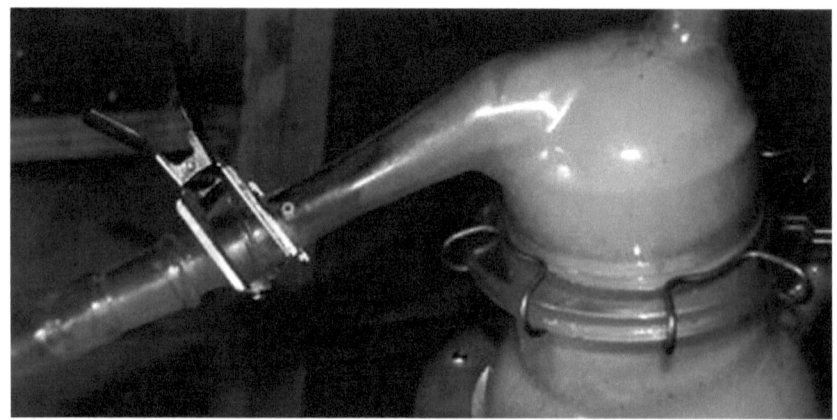

Fig.118: Modern glass alembic head with the fixing rings on the spout.

We find the same rings in the Pakistan (Fig. 119) specimens published by Allchin (see chapter VII, 47) as well as on some modern devices employed to produce pharmacological compounds (Fig. 118). In addition, through experimentations made with the 1/1 replica of a set, it was possible to distil 35 litres (measure corresponding to the capacity of the jar used as cucurbit) in about 3-4 hours, stating that we could accelerate or slow the distillation disconnecting the spout from the neck of the jug (collector).

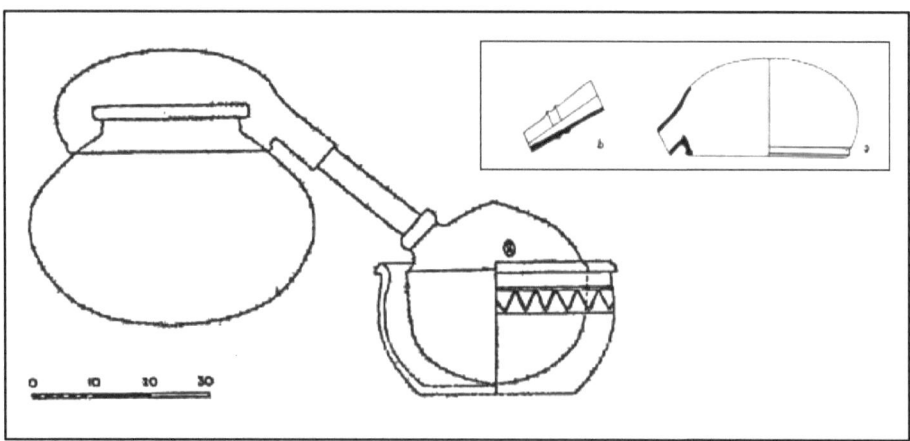

Fig. 119: Shaikhan Dherì: reconstruction of distilling apparatus from Allchin 1979.

In this case, although slowed, the distillation continues and the condensation of the steam drops directly from the spout, with a different concentration of essential oil. In turn, leaving all the vapour going inside the jug we found at the end one-centimetre of essential oil floating above the condensed liquid. To the recovering of this oil we have associated the clay funnels found not far from the devices, probably employed in this operation as they have today. The same funnel is visible in the photo of the alembic set found in Pakistan at Sirkap in the Indus Valley in the exhibition at the Museum of Taxila in Pakistan (Fig. 120), which in 1970 took the attention of the chemist Paolo Rovesti[127], who, believing it dates to the 2000 BC and ignoring it was still published (Marshall 1951), announced he had found the most ancient alembic of the world.

Unfortunately, the levels of Taxila where J. Marshall found the objects (not in the same room) dates to the 3rd - 2nd century BC[128].

Fig. 120: Taxila apparatus assembled by Marshall from objects found in the excavations of Taxila (funnel in the flask), photo taken in the Museum by P. Rovesti in 1970.

---

[127] P. Rovesti 1980. Alla scoperta del primo alambicco del mondo: la distillazione ha cinquemila anni. Rivista Italiana *EPPOS*, LXII, n°7 342-345.
[128] Marshall, J. (1951) *Taxila* (3 v.) 420, Cambridge; for distiller employ see also: Ray 1956, 80; Mahdihassan 1972, 164.

Many other specimens found in the valley of Peshavar at Shaikhan Dheri (Fig. 119) in levels dating back between 150 BC to 350 A.D [129] have been studied and published by Allchin, who noticed some pots reporting engraved ideograms similar to those incised on the handles of the large basin of Pyrgos.

Fig.121: a, ideograms on the handle of the basin n°131, and b, Allchin ideogram class M, according to the comparison table (below Fig. 122).

The comparison of the ideograms of Pyrgos with those of the Allchin has revealed a surprising affinity, having a part of the ideogram composed by a similar sequence (Fig. 121, Fig. 122).

Even if we consider the distance in time, the resemblance is undeniable suggesting that part of the ideogram could symbolize distillation and its first use to identify the function of an apparatus may have Cypriot origin.

The fact is quite curious, but coincides with the well-known survival of chemical and alchemical symbols through the millennia, such as the chalice with a snake wrapped around the stem that symbolizes medicine.

---

[129] F.R. Allchin 1979. Evidence of Early Distillation at Shaikhan Dheri" in M. Taddei ed. *South Asian Archaeology* 1977, vol. I, Istituto Univ. Orientale, Napoli.

STRATUM																		
I																		
II				4													23	27,28, 30,32
III					5								13	14,15, 19			26	
IV						6	7,11	8	9	10	12			16,17 18,20	21	22	24,25	29,31
V																		
VI																		
VII	1	2	3															
VIII																		
IX																		
X, XI																		
	丌	帀	三	靣	中	㐃	英	千	丣	丵	㚣	天	㒸	丮	〒	㞢	屮
CLASS	A	B	C	D	E	F	G	H	J	K	L	M	N	O	P	Q	R

Fig.122: Comparison table of ideograms engraved on Peshavar pots: by Allchin 1979.

The depiction goes back to the VI c. BC, referring to Hygiea, daughter of Aesculapius (Asclepius), powerful divine physician and son of Apollo, represented with a snake or a glass in hand, on which the sacred snake wraps.

Since the classical period the ideogram of the calyx with a snake has been used to identify places, people and objects relating to medicine, and Hygeia representation as a girl holding snakes, reminds the well-known Minoan figurines of the lady with the snakes in her hands, curiously turning us back to the 2000 BC Crete.

Finally, it is possible that the sequence described by Allchin represents the evolution of an ideogram born in the Mediterranean, indicating the purpose of the object and not its ownership. In short, it could symbolize distillation. Although it is difficult to prove the survival of such an ideogram throughout the centuries, there is no doubt that the two symbols reported by Antoine-Joseph Pernety in 1758 in his *Dictionnaire Mytho-*

hermétique seem to be a direct evolution from the Pyrgos one: *Distillation (Virgo)* and *Separation (Scorpio)* (Fig. 123)[130].

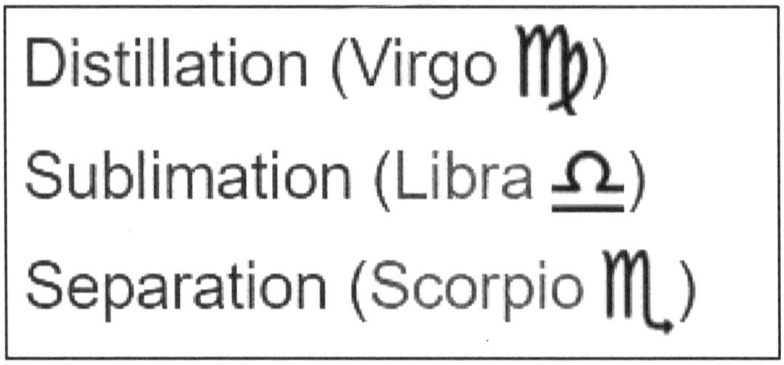

> Distillation (Virgo ♍)
> Sublimation (Libra ♎)
> Separation (Scorpio ♏)

Fig. 123: Alchemical symbols associated with the distillation process and Zodiac Constellations according to A.J. Pernety Dictionnaire mytho-hermétique.

The first corresponding to distillation and Virgo constellation (water) is composed of three vertical lines joined at the top, and a fourth line folded, crossing the extremity of the third.

The second corresponding to the separation and the constellation of Scorpio is like the first, missing the fourth line. The alchemical meaning is very similar. In turn, completely different is the symbol and the meaning of the sublimation which appears in connection with the constellation of Libra (scales-balance).

The symbol consists of two parallels signs, straight lower and straight with a medium semicircle the upper, schematically summarize the sublimation process of the minerals (that is the "separation" of the components) by superimposing a closed container to a flat surface as in the drawing of Needham (before Fig.6). The preservation of the symbolism of these ideograms through the centuries confirms that the art of distillation moved many times up and down the circum-Mediterranean

---

[130] Pernety. Antoine-Joseph 1758 : *Dictionnaire mytho-hermétique, dans lequel on trouve les allégories fabuleuses des poètes, les métaphores, les énigmes et les termes barbares des philosophes hermétiques expliqués.* 99, Paris.

area and Middle East, the region that became the home of the most famous alchemists of the medieval period, transcribing in Arabic much of the millenarian Mediterranean wisdom.

Replica of the Pyrgos Alembic by Andrea Phasoulides working during an exhibition at Korakou (Nicosia) Cyprus, in 2012.

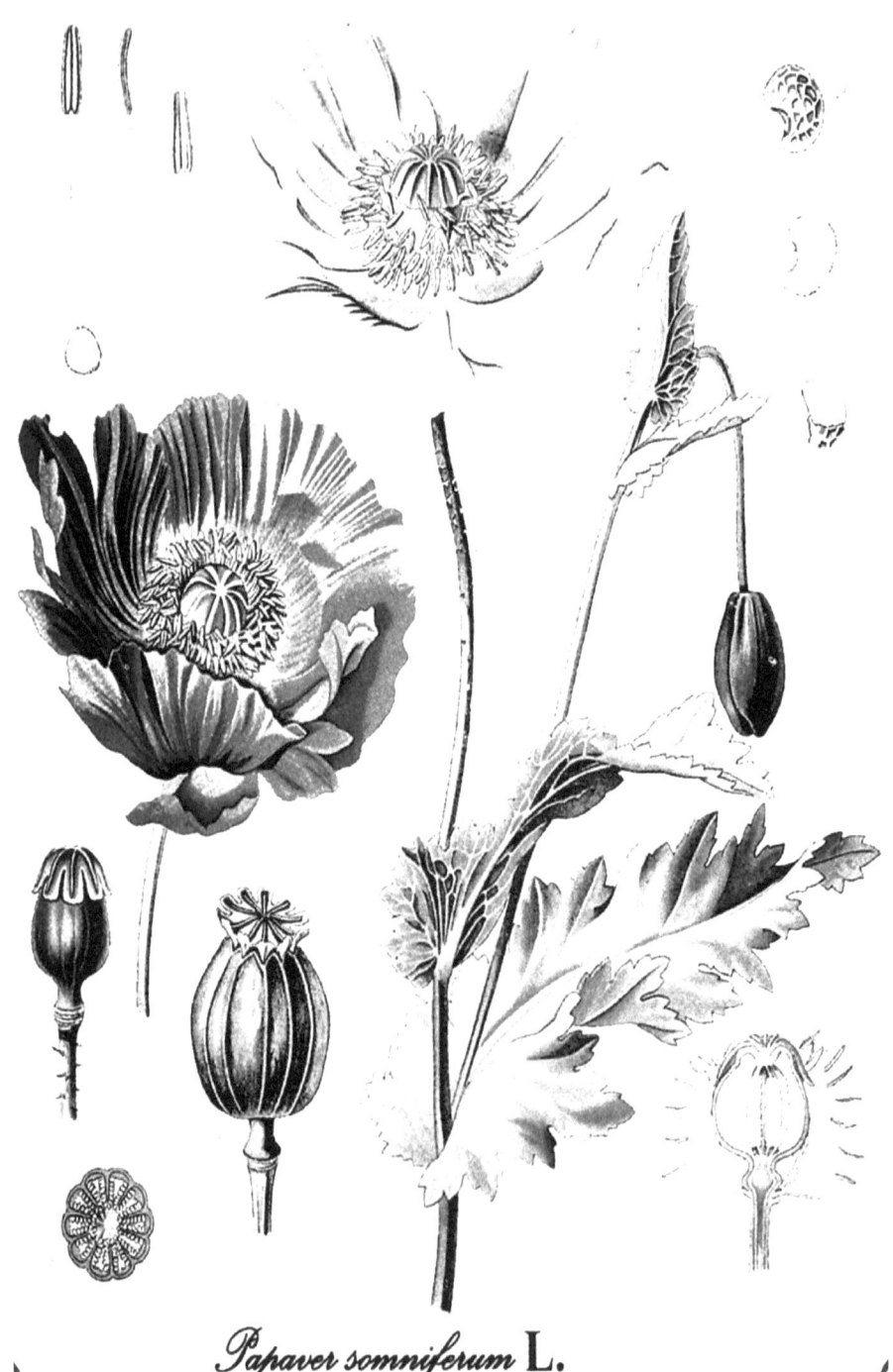

Papaver somniferum L.

XIV. A final reflection.

Writing this short research, I took the belief that distillation has been considered in antiquity a philosophy more than a technology. A sort of magic procedure to obtain substances giving pleasure and health of humans.

Of course, they never considered distillation the sublimation of the inorganic substances and metalloids, until the first centuries AD, although according to the laws of physics the phenomenon is a direct passage from the gaseous state to the liquid or from the gaseous to the solid is similar.

The amount of organic and inorganic materials that are now being processed through distillation is enormous. In fact, very few are the objects around us that do not include ingredients are obtained through distillation. Just think about fuels, plastics and all the chemical and organic substances used in the pharmaceutical, cosmetic, and domestic fields.

The products we use today are not very different from the old ones, and even if you don't realize it, their composition and extraction has had to rely on distillation processes which, although primitive, were still valid. Among the most important ingredients of which we have evidence of use, are resins oleoresins, and gums [131], widely used as adhesives, waterproofing, beverage flavourings, preservatives, components of medicines, and disinfectants.

---

[131] Regarding Cyprus: Lardos A, Prieto-Garcia J, Heinrich M. Resins and Gums in Historical *Iatrosophia* Texts from Cyprus – A Botanical and Medico-pharmacological Approach. *Frontiers in Pharmacology*. 2011; 2: 32. doi:10.3389/fphar.2011. 00032.

Most of the last century studies regarding the history of distillation and the evolution of apparatuses described devices for chemical experiments[132] pointing to separate metals or minerals to make new compositions and study their reactions, few were used really for pharmaceutical compounds, essential oils, or scented waters. Of course, the distillation could refer to both extractions of essential oil and spirit, necessary to produce pharmaceutical tinctures.

For example, Mahdihassan bases his research on the knowledge of wine and spirit distillation in India in 1500 BC[133]. The scholar examines various testimonies about the distillation, mentioning cross-references of the Vedic texts that seem to refer to still processes[134]. The subject is of some interest, particularly the context in which were found devices in the Aegean and Cyprus, and especially in consideration with the grape pips found around, which unfortunately are not sufficient to confirm the hypothesis.

Conversely, the presence of funnels in the same contexts suggests the process was addressed to produce hydrosol and essential oils.

Meanwhile, in the Medieval period the distillation of alcohol and alcoholic liquors, which are not represented in the illustrations of the time, and not included in canonical Alchemical investigations, was probably the most widespread use involving alembics in private and rural environment.

The recent discovery in Bulgaria of a spout and fragments of a clay vessel

---

[132] T.F. Sherwood 1945: The evolution of the Still, in *ANS*, 5, 185.

[133] S. Mahdihassan 1972: The earliest Distillation units of pottery in Indo-Pakistan in *Pakistan Archaeology* (v.8), 161-168;
- S. Mahdihassan 1979: Distillation assembly of pottery in ancient India with a single item of special construction. *Vishveshvaranand Indological Journal* vol. 17, 264.
- S. Mahdihassan 1981: Parisrut the earliest distilled liquor of Vedic times or of about 1500 BC, *Indian J Hist Sci*. Vol. 16 Issue 2, Nov 1981, 223-229.

[134] S. Mahdihassan 1991: The word Kohala in Susruta and Term Alcool-Vini of Paracelsus, *Indian Journal of History of Science*, 26 (2), 131-132.

for *Rakia* distillation dating back the 11th century is one case[135].

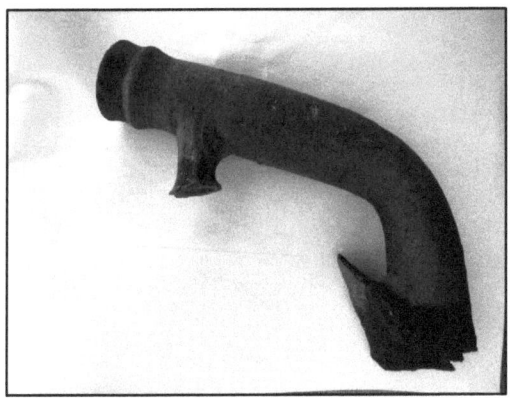

Fig. 124: Spout of a *Rakia* distillation vessel of the 11th century found in 2015 at Ivaylovgrad Lyutitsa Fortress, Bulgaria.

Perfumes, spirits, potions, and pharmaceutical compounds had a fundamental role in the history and they are connected not only with a specific "apparatus", but with an appropriate interpretation of life, nature, magic, and religion. The laboratories, their equipment and spatial location had a special meaning often involving personal power and divine protection, which are the factors ever present in the archaeological environments from which the specimens dating back to the prehistory of distillation belong. We should consider these objects not as an isolated case, but as instruments of a precise outfit located in a place arranged to produce specific substances on demand. Something not far from the medieval alchemical laboratory: a large room with dry plants and part of animals hung on the walls and on the ceiling, recipes on the table, amulets to grant the success, baskets full of minerals, store jars of principal liquids (water, oil, wine), vases containing fragrances and special ingredients, mortars and pestles, palettes, pit furnaces, pot stands, cooking pots, spouted bowls, funnels, strainers, and jugs. A confusion of different

---

[135] Spout of a *rakia* distillation vessel of the 11th century found in 2015 at Ivaylovgrad Lyutitsa Fortress, Bulgaria.
http://archaeologyinbulgaria.com/2015/07/27/archaeologists-find-fragment-of-11th-century-rakia-distillation-vessel-in-lyutitsa-fortress-near-bulgarias-ivaylovgrad/

objects and materials that finds its order and reason only with the people working there.

It is only after the presence of these outfits that you can recognize an ancient laboratory destroyed or abandoned for centuries (the case of Pyrgos/Mavroraki). In these terms, the discarding of all the fragmentary material of Tepe Gawra during the excavation, without even counting the number of the pots room by room, can be considered a serious loss of cultural heritage, since the context was more important than the specimens.

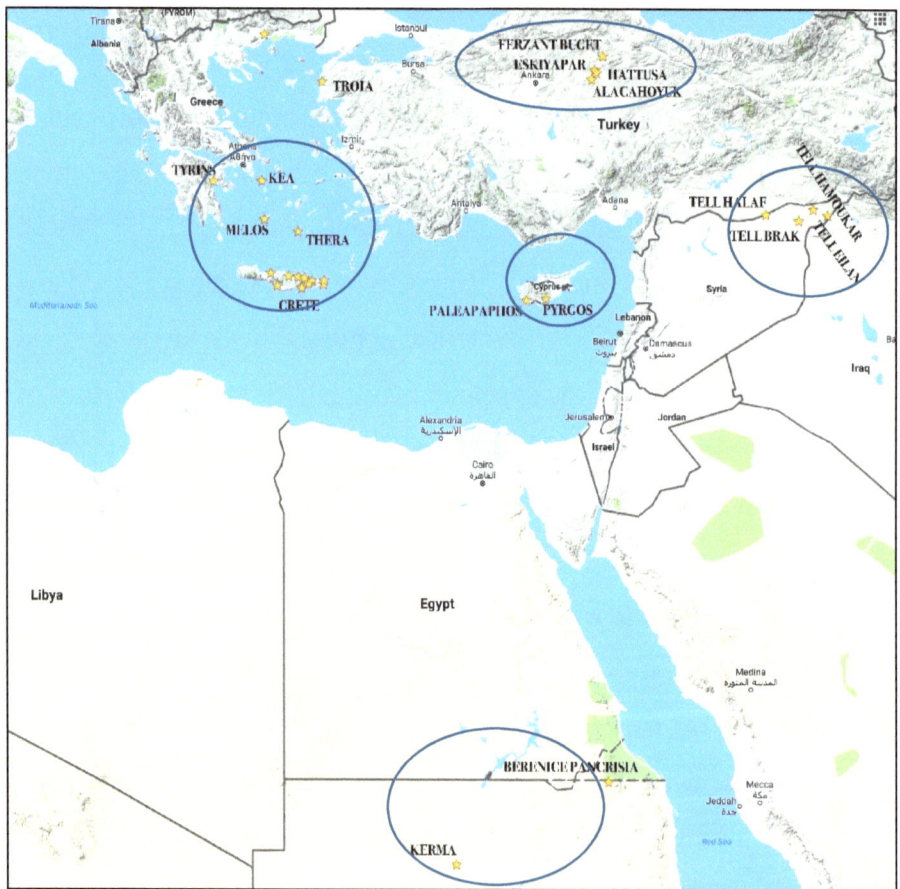

Fig. 125: Geographic areas involved in producing prototypes for distillation.

The only evidence that we can connect to the 12 Tepe Gawra channel pots is the presence of a tripartite temple, which occupied a large portion of the small village (just one hectare), inhabited by 150-200 people, whose abnormal wealth suggests a productive activity connected in some manner with pilgrims visiting the holy place. For a very long time, the technique of direct recycling distillation coming from Mesopotamia has probably joined simple distillation, made with spouted pots and funnels, which have never been considered components of a set to distil, giving them typological importance only in local pottery evolution.

Unfortunately, the discovery of pottery, modified as a component of distillation apparatus, has often been considered in an isolated case, while the archaeological experience teaches us that there are no unique pieces, but ceramic typologies that have evolved in the breast to precise cultural evolution, involving large territories, and remaining for a long-time span.

This is the case of Tepe Gawra and its channel pots of the Ubaid period found in many sites and existing also in a spouted version; of the Cycladic tureen strainer pots, known in dozens of specimens, extant in the Aegean for at least eight centuries; of the spouted bowls of the High Nubia characteristics of the so-called Kerma period B; of the fakes Hittite teapots found in Hattusa and other sites, and of the Cyprus spouted pots producing on the island in the most bizarre versions since the Early Bronze age.

All the pots have a specific position in the local typological repertoire, and in two cases, Tepe Gawra and Crete, they became so important to be reproduced in miniature model for the funeral outfit. In this regard, we can see the miniature pots, objects that transfers and retains the acquired experience in time and space. Furthermore, if Mesopotamia may be considered an isolated phenomenon of the late 4th millennium BC, even though it involved a large area of the upper Valley of the Tigris and a temporal space of at least three centuries, the almost simultaneously advent at the beginning of the 2nd millennium BC of different technological solutions in Anatolia, Aegean islands, Cyprus and Nubia could not be considered a case, but the real birthday of distillation in a circum-Mediterranean area involved in traffics of wealth and ephemeral goods (Fig. 125). If we compare, in the limits of the published archaeological evidence, the number of clay specimens dating back 2000/1000 BC with the number of clay, glass and copper specimens of the Medieval period dating back $1/15^{th}$ century AD, we realize how difficult it has been to find workshops and objects in Medieval contexts than in sites of the Bronze age, as the case of fragmentary Bulgarian spouts suggests (i.e. Fig. 124). Fortunately, from the Medieval period, we have transcriptions and copies of drawings in manuscripts that make up for the lack of objects, confirming, that the laboratories, that we can eventually call alchemical, were just like David Teniers painted in 1600 (Fig. 126).

Fig. 126: David Teniers the Younger - Herzog Anton Ulrich-Museum Braunschweig 1643.

Me and Theodosia Yankou from Aghia Irini (Kyrenia), a friendship dating to 1971.

REFERENCES

- Al Quntar S., Khalidi L., and J. Ur 2011: Proto-Urbanism in The Late 5th Millennium BC: Survey and Excavations at Khirbat Al-Fakhar (Hamoukar), Northeast Syria, In: *Paléorient,* vol. 37, n°2. 151-175.

- Abu al-Soof B. 1967: More soundings at Tell Qalinj Agha (Erbil) in *Sumer* 23: 69-75.

- Abu al Soof B. 1969: Excavations at Tell Qalinj Agha (Erbil) Summer1968, in *Sumer* 25: 3-42.

- Allchin F.R. 1979a: India: the ancient home of distillation?, *Man*, vol. 14, 55-63.

- Allchin F.R. 1979b: Evidence of early distillation at Shaikhān Dheri, in: M. Taddei (cur.), *South Asian Archaeology 1977*, Istituto Orientale, Napoli, 755-797.

- Andersson J.G. 1947: Prehistoric sites in Honan. In: *BM FEA*,19, I. *Bulletin no. 19 of the Museum of Far Eastern Antiquities*.

- Antona A., Corro M.D.M. and S. Puggioni 2010: Spazi di Lavoro e Attività Produttive nel Villaggio Nuragico la Prisgiona in località Capichera (Arzachena), in: M. Milanese et al. (Cur.), *L'africa Romana*, Vol. III, Carocci Editore, Roma, 1713-1734.

- Arnaud de Villeneuve 1309: *De conservanda juventute, ac retardanda senectute* (Londres, British Mus. Sloane) in: Berthelot, *Ann Chim Phys*. 1891, 6èmc série, t. XXII, 469-475.

- Arnold J.P. 1911: *Origin and History of Beer and Brewing,* Chicago.

- Aristoteles *Météorology*. Translation in Peter L. Schoonheim, *Aristotle's Meteorology in the Arabico-Latin Tradition*, (Leiden: Brill) 2000.

- Baily J. 1973: *The God-Kings & the Titans,* St. Martin's Press.

- Bartholomew J. 2015: Bronze Age Alcohol distillation or extraction for aromas and tastes. Poster at *Experimental Archaeology Conference 9,* University college, Dublin.

- Bartoli A. & Cappelletti C. 2007: Antiquitates: Tecniche di archeologia sperimentale applicate alla riproduzione dei profumi, in M.R. Belgiorno, (a cura di) *I Profumi di Afrodite e il segreto dell'Olio*, Gangemi, Roma, 137-145.

- Bartoli A., Belgiorno M.R., Cappelletti C. and A. Lentini 2009: *Cipro: Un Sito di 4000 Anni fa e l'Archeologia Sperimentale*, Collana I Quaderni di Antiquitates, ed. Tuscia, Viterbo.

- Behrens G. 1952: Römische Milchkocher. In *Anzeiger der Römisch-Germanischen Kommission des Deutschen Archäologischen Instituts Frankfurt*, M: Henrich-ed., Vol. 30, No. 1, 110-111.

- Belgiorno M.R. 2016: *The Perfume of Cyprus.* Roma Ermes.

- Belgiorno M.R. 2017a: Subject Presentation: Pyrgos/Mavroraki, in M.R. Belgiorno (Ed), *Archaeometry and Aphrodite* Proceedings of the seminar 13th June 2013 CNR Rome, 1-34.

- Belgiorno M.R. 2017b: Cosmetics, in M.R. Belgiorno (Ed), *Archaeometry and Aphrodite Proceedings of the seminar 13th June 2013 CNR Rome*, 45-93.

- Belgiorno M.R. & A. Lentini 2008a: A. Paleoethnobotany investigations at the site of Pyrgos-Mavroraki, Cyprus, *International Symposium on Archaeometry*, Kars H., Meyers P. and Wagner C.A. Editors, 37. Siena, 296-297.

- Belgiorno M.R. & A. Lentini 2008b: Image Analysis and Measurement Applied to the Archaeological Material from Pyrgos (Cyprus), in *Remote Sensing in Archaeology and the Management of Cultural Heritage*, Lasaponara R. and Masini N. Eds, Aracne Editrice, Roma. 419-423.

- Belgiorno M.R. e Lentini A. 2010: Monitoraggio aerobiologico dei pollini, spore e microresti vegetali, nell'area archeologica di Pyrgos/Mavrorachi (Cipro), *Il Monitoraggio costiero Mediterraneo: Problematiche e Tecniche di Misura*, a cura di Benincasa F., CNR-IBIMET, 257-276, Firenze.

- Berthelot M. 1887: Collection Des Anciens Alchimistes Grecs, in *Bibliotheca Chemica de Manget* 540, T. I; reprint Genève, 1702.

- Berthelot M. 1887: Figures des appareils des alchimistes grecs. *Annales de Chimie et de Physique.* Paris.

- Berthelot M. 1889: *Introduction à l'étude de la Chimie des Anciens et du Moyen Age*, Steinheil Paris.

- Berthelot M. 1892: *Revue des deux mondes*, Paris.

- Berthelot M. 1893: *La chimie au moyen âge*, Imprimerie nationale. Paris.

- Bignasca A.M. 2000: *I kernoi circolari in Oriente e in Occidente. Strumenti di culto e immagini cosmiche*, Universitätsverlag Freibueg Schweiz Vandenhoeck & Ruprecht Göttingen.

- Birrell A. 1999: *Chinese Mythology: An Introduction*, J. Hopkins ed. JHU.

- Bolzan J. E. 1976: Chemical Combination According to Aristotles, in *Ambix* 23: 134-44.

- Bosanquet R.C. & Dawkins R. McG. 1923: *The unpublished objects from the Palaikastro excavations*, 1902-1906, Macmillan & co. BSA.

- Bourke J.G. 1893: Primitive Distillation among the Tarascoes. In *American Anthropologist*, A. 6: 65–70.

- Boyd Hawes H., Williams B.E., Seager R.B. and Hall E.H. 1908: *Gournia, Vasiliki and Other Prehistoric Sites on the Isthmus of Hierapetra, Crete. Excavations of the Wells- Houston- Cramp Expeditions, 1901, 1903, 1904*, Philadelphia.

- Brenning M. 1904: *Nikanders Theriaka und Alexipharmaka*. Allgemeine medizinische Central-Zeitung.

- Brunschwig Hieronymus 1500: *Liber de arte distillandi de simplicibus*. et 1512: *Liber de arte distillandi de compositis*. Strasbourg.

- Butler A.R. and Needham J. 1980: An Experimental Comparison of the East Asian, Hellenistic and Indian (Gandharan) Stills in Relation to the Distillation of Ethanol and Acetic Acid, "*Ambix*" XXVII 69-76.

- Campus F. & Leonelli V. 2000: *La tipologia della ceramica nuragica. Il materiale edito*, Beta Gamma edizioni.

- Carinci F. 2011: Strumentazioni per il Filtraggio nei Contesti di Apparato del Primo Palazzo di Festòs in *Kretes Minoidos. Tradizione e identità minoica tra produzione artigianale, pratiche cerimoniali e memoria del passato,* Studi offerti a V. La Rosa 103-116. Padova.

- Charas M. 1691: *Pharmacopée royale Galénique et chymique.* Tome 1. Paris, chez -Laurent d' Houry.

- Chaptal J. A. 1823: *Chimie appliquée à l'agriculture.*Tome 1. Paris, chez Madame Huzard.

- Curry A. 2016: *The Alchemist's Tale.* In: *Archaeology*, Magazine, Jan/Feb 2016, Vol. 69 Issue 1, 36.

- Dandekar R.N. 2005: subject in, *Encyclopaedia of Religion*, Mac Millaned vol. XIV, 9550, New York.

- Dani A. H. 1966: Shaikhan Dheri excavations, 1963 and 1964, in *Ancient Pakistan 2*: 17-214. Peshawar.

- Dawkins, R. 1903: Pottery from Zakro. In: *The Journal of Hellenic Studies*, 23, 248-260.

- Δημοπουλου Ν. 2005: Ρεθεμιωτακη, *Το Αρχαιολογικό Μουσείο Ηρακλείου.*

- Diels H. 1879: *Doxographi Graeci*, Berlin.

- Dietler M. 2006: Alcohol: Anthropological/Archaeological Perspectivesin, in: *Annual Review of Anthropology 35*: 1, 229-249.

- Dikaios P. & J.R. Stewart 1962: *The Swedish Cyprus Expedition* vol. IV, part 1A, Lund.

- Dioscourides Pedanios, *De Materia medica.* Translation J. Berendes 1902.

- El Khadem H.S. 1996: A Translation of a Zosimos Text in an Arabic Alchemy Book, in *Journal of the Washington Academy of Sciences* vol. 84, 168-178.

- Fairley Y. 1907: The Early History of Distillation, in: *Journal of the institute of brewing*, vol. 13, 559-582.

- Fink C.G. & Kopp A.H. 1933: Ancient Antimony Plating on Copper Objects in *Met. Mus. Studies* 4, 163-67. Stockholm.

- Fischer F. 1963: Die hethitische Keramik von Boğazköy. *Boğazköy-Hattuša* 4, Berlin.

- Forbes R.J. 1948: *A short history of the art of distillation*, e.j. Brill, Leiden.

- Forbes R.J. 1948: *Studies in Ancient Technology (= SAT) VI*, Leiden 1948.

- French J. 1651: *The art of Distillation or a Treatise of the Choicest Spagyricall Preparations performed by way of Distillation with the Description of the Chiefest Furnaces and Vessels used by Ancient and Moderne Chymists*, 17 ss. London: T. Williams, Six Books.

- Friedrich P. 1982: *The Meaning of Aphrodite,* The University of Chicago Press.

- Georgiou H.S. 1980: Minoan Fireboxes: A Study of Form and Function, in *SMEA* 21, 123-187.

- Georgiou H.S. 1986: *Keos VI, Ayia Irini. Specialized and Industrial Pottery*, 43. Mainz.

- Grahan J. 2000. Foreword in: Betty De Shong Meador, *Lady of Largest Heart: poems of the Sumerian high priestess Enheduann*a, University of Texas Press.

- Gwei-Djen Lu, Needham J. & Needham D. 1972, The coming of ardent water, *Ambix*, vol. 19, 69-112.

- Glauber J.R 1658: *Descriptio artis distillatoriæ novae*, Amsterdam.

- Gorreus J. 1549: *Nicandri Colophonii Alexipharmaca. Io. Gorraeo Parisiensi medico interprete. Eiusdem interpretis in Alexipharmaca praefatio, omnem de uenenis disputationem summatim complectens, & annotationes*. Parisiis, apud Vascosanum via Iacobaea, ad insigne Fontis.

- Halbherr F., Stefani E. & L. Banti 1977: *Haghia Triada nel periodo tardo palaziale*, AS Atene 55 (n.s. 39).

- Handwerk B. 2009: Scorpion King's Wines Egypt's Oldest, Spiked with Meds, in *National Geographic News* April 13.

- Harman A. 2015: *Harvest to Hydrosol,* IAG Botanics LLC dba bot AN Nicals Fruitland, WA 99129.

- Hartmann L.F. and Oppenheim A.L. 1950: *On Beer and Brewing Techniques in Ancient Mesopotamia* in: JAOS Suppl. 10.

- Hoefer F. 1866: *Histoire de la chimie.* Didot, Paris. Tome 1.

- Hogarth D.G. 1900-1901: Excavations at *Zakro*, Crete, *BSA* V: 129-141.

- Hogarth D.G. 1902: Bronze-Age Vases from Zakro. - *Journal of Hellenic Studies* 22: 333.

- Hurry Jamieson B. 1926: *Imhotep, the Vizier and Physician of King Zoser and Afterwards the Egyptian God of Medicine,* London, Oxford University Press.

- Hyppolytus, *"Philosophoumena"* Liber IV- cap. 31, Latin version *"Refutatio omnium haeresium"*, translated by Hermann Diels Doxographi Graeci, 306, Berlin, 1879.

- Jabir ibn ayyan Hayyan (Geber) 1531: *De alchimia, libri tres*, Argentorati. Bibliotheca Complutense, fondo historico. Madrid.

- James P.A. & D.T. Mininberg 2005*: The Art of Medicine in Ancient Egypt.* Exhibition at The Metropolitan Museum of Art, New York.

- Jayyab K.A. 2012: A Ceramic Chronology from Tell Hamoukar Southern Extension, 95. in C. Marro ed. *After the Ubaid: Interpreting Change from the Caucasus to Mesopotamia at the Dawn of Urban Civilization* (4500-3500 BC): *Papers from the post-Ubaid Horizon in the Fertile Crescent and Beyond, International Workshop held at Fosseuse, 29th June-1st July 2009.*Varia Anatolica XXVII, 87-129 Paris.

- Kerckring T. 1671: *Commentarius in currum triumphalem Antimonii Basilii Valentini.* Amsterdam.

- Keyser P.T. & James S.R. 1989: "Hominid Use of Fire in the Lower and Middle Pleistocene: A Review of the Evidence,", in: *Current Anthropology* 30, 1-26.

- Karageroghis V. 1990: *Tombs at Palaeopaphos. 1. Teratsoudhia. 2. Eliomylia*, A.G. Leventis Foundation, Nicosia.

- Kriga D. 2014: Flora and Fauna Iconography on Strainers and Kymbai at Akrotiri: Theran Ceramic Vessels of Special Use and Special Iconography *499-505, in* Aegaeum 37: *Actes de la 14e Rencontre égéenne internationale, Paris, Institut National d'Histoire de l'Art (INHA)* 11-14 décembre 2012.

- Lancillotti C. 1681: *Nuova guida alla chimica, che per suo mezzo conduce gl'affetionati alle operazioni sopra ogni corpo misto animale, minerale ò vegetabile...* Venetia.

- Lardos A, Prieto-Garcia J, Heinrich M. 2011: Resins and Gums in Historical *Iatrosophia* Texts from Cyprus – A Botanical and Medico-pharmacological Approach. *Frontiers in Pharmacology.* 2: 32.

- Lavoisier A.L. 1792: *System der antiphologistischen Chemie.* Aus dem Französischen übersetzt und mit Anmerkungen und Zusätzen versehen von D. Sigismund Friedrich Hermbstädt. 2 Bde in 1.8° Berlin

- Lentini A. & Scala G. 2004: Fragrant substances and therapeutic compounds, in: Belgiorno M.R. (ed), *Pyrgos/Mavrorachi <Advanced Technology in Bronze Age Cyprus>*, 45-47, CNR Bureau President's, Nicosia.

- Lentini A. & G. Scala 2006: Aromatic and therapeutic substances from the prehistoric site of Pyrgos-Mavrorachi (Cyprus), in: Belgiorno M.R. (ed), *Cyprus Aromata, Olive Oil in Perfumery and Medicaments in Cyprus 2000 B.C.*, Edizioni Eranuova, Perugia 2006, 219-243.

- Lentini A. & G. Scala 2007: Sostanze odorose e terapeutiche dal sito Preistorico di Pyrgos/Mavrorachi: indagini chimico tossicologiche e archeo botaniche preliminari; in: Belgiorno M.R. *Il Profumo di Afrodite e il Segreto dell'Olio*, 87-109, Gangemi Editore, Roma.

- Lentini A. & M.R. Belgiorno 2008: Palaethnobotany investigations at the site of Pyrgos-Mavrorachi, Cyprus, in Kars H., Meyers P., and Wagner C.A. (ed.) *International Symposium on Archaeometry*, 37, 296-297.

- Lentini A. & Nelli M. 2008: Schede delle specie officinali identificate nel sito Preistorico di Pyrgos/Mavrorachi (Cipro), in Belgiorno M.R.

(ed), *Mavrorachi – Dal 2000 ad oggi quattromila anni di profumo*, Gangemi Editore, Roma,110-135.

- Lentini A. 2009: Archeologia e paesaggio naturale: indagini archeo botaniche e fisico chimiche, in: M.R. Belgiorno (ed), *Cipro all'inizio dell'Età del Bronzo. Realtà sconosciute della comunità industriale di Pyrgos/Mavroraki*, Gangemi Editore, Roma, 128-187.

- Lentini A. 2010: Scents in the ancient civilizations of the Mediterranean basin: archaeometric studies on Cleopatra's officine (En Boqeq, Israel) and on Pyrgos/Mavroraki's perfumery (Cyprus), in M.R. Belgiorno, Lazarou Y. and Lentini A. *Perfume de Chypre, The role of Aphrodite's island in the history of the Mediterranean scents*, F. Lazarou Investiment LTD, Nicosia, 105 - 153.

- Lentini A. 2017: Archaeometry, in M.R. Belgiorno (Ed), *Archaeometry and Aphrodite* Proceedings of the seminar 13th June 2013 CNR Rome 95-143.

- Levi D. & F. Carinci 1988: *Festòs e la Civiltà Minoica*, II.2 *Incunabula Graeca* 77, Roma.

- Levey M. 1955: Evidences of ancient distillation, sublimation and extraction in Mesopotamia, in *Centaurus*, T IV: 22-33.

- Levey M. 1960: A Group of Akkadian Texts on Perfumery in M. Levey 1960. *Early Muslim Chemistry: its debt to Ancient Babylonia,* in *Chymia*, Annual Studies in the History of Chemistry, University of Pennsylvania Press, H.M. Leicester ed. Vol.6, Philadelphia.

- Levey M. 1973: *Early Arabic Pharmacology: An Introduction Based on Ancient and Medieval Sources,* Leiden.

- Li H.R. 1995: *The Chinese alcoholic culture Shanxi People's* Publishing House, Taiyuan [In Chinese].

- Liang Shih-cheng 1751 (1888): *Hsi Chhing Ku Chien 170. Catalogue of Ancient Mirrors and Bronzes of the Imperial Collection in the Library of Western Serenity.* Shanghai 1888.

- Liebmann A.J. 1956: History of Distillation, *Journal of Chemical Education*, Vol. 33, 166-173.

- Libavii A. (Poet Physici) 1597: *Alchemiae*, Rotemburg, Francofurti, Iohannes Saurius.

- Liverani M. 2006: *Uruk la prima città*, Laterza, Roma.

- Needham J. 1980: *Science and Civilisation in China, vol. V, Chemistry and Chemical Technology. Part IV: Spagyrical Discovery and Invention: Apparatus, Theories and Gifts.* Cambridge Un. Press

- Mahdihassan S. 1972: The Earliest Distillation Units Of Pottery In Indo-Pakistan, *Pakistan Archaeology*, Vol. 8, 161-8.

- Mahdihassan S. 1979: Distillation Assembly Of Pottery In Ancient India With A Single Item Of Special Construction, *Vishveshvaranand Indological Journal*, Vol. 17, 264-266.

- Mahdihassan S. 1981: *Parisrut*, The Earliest Distilled Liquor Of Vedic Times Or Of About 1500 B.C., *Indian Journal Of History Of Science*, Vol. 16, 223-229.

- Mahdihassan S. 1991: The word Kohala in Susruta and Term Alcool-Vini of Paracelsus, in *Indian Journal of History of Science*, 26 (2), 131-132.

- Marinatos S. 1969: *Excavations at Thera II (1968 season)*; Athēnais Archaiologikē Hetaireia, Athens.

- Marinatos S. 1974: *Excavations at Thera VI (1972 season);* Athēnais Archaiologikē Hetaireia, Athens.

- Marshall J. 1951: *Taxila.* 3 vols. Cambridge.

- Martelli M. 2011: Greek Alchemists at Work: Alchemical Laboratory, in the Greco-Roman Egypt, *Nuncius* 26, 271–311.

- Martini W. 2010: *Die Akropolis von Perge in Pamphylien – vom Siedlungsplatz zur Akropolis*, Stuttgart.

- Martinon-Torres M. 2012: The Archaeology of Alchemy and Chemistry in the Early Modern World: an afterthought in: *Archaeology International* No. 15, 2011-2012, 33-36.

- Matthews R. (ed.) 2001: *Excavations at Tell Brak 4: Exploring an Upper Mesopotamian Regional Centre, 1994-1996.* McDonald Institute Monographs, Cambridge.

- McGovern, P. E., Hartung U., Badler V.R., Glusker D.L. and L.J. Exner 1997: The Beginnings of Winemaking and Viniculture in the Ancient Near East and Egypt. *Expedition* 39 (1): 3–21.

- McGovern P.E., Zhang J., Tang J., Zhang Z., Hall G.R., Moreau R.A., Nun~ez A., Butrym E.D., Richards M.P., Wang C-shan, Cheng G., Zhao Z., and C. Wang 2004: Fermented beverages of pre- and proto-historic China, in *PNAS*, vol. 101 no. 51.

- McGovern P.E., Glusker D.L., Exner L.J. and G.R. Hall 2008: The Chemical Identification of Resinated Wine and a Mixed Fermented Beverage in Bronze-Age Pottery Vessels of Greece, in *Archaeology Meets Science: Biomolecular Investigations in Bronze age Greece; The Primary Scientific Evidence, 1997-2003,* ed. Y. Tzedakis et al-, 169-218. Oxford: Oxbow.

- McGovern P.E., Mirzoian, A., Hall G.R. 2009: Ancient Egyptian herbal wines, *Proc Natl Acad Sci U S A. May 5*; 106(18): 7361–7366. Published online 2009 Apr 13. Doi: 10. 1073/ pnas.0811578106.

- Moorhouse S. 1972: Medieval distilling apparatus of glass and pottery. With an introduction by F. Greenaway, *Medieval Archaeology*, 16, 79-121.

- Morewood S. 1824: *An essay on the inventions and customs of both ancients and moderns in the use of inebriating liquors, interspersed with interesting anecdotes, illustrative of the manners and habits of the principal nations of the world, with a historical view of the extent practice of distillation, both as it relates to commerce and as a source of national income, comprising much curious information respecting the application and properties of several parts of the vegetable kingdom,* Longman, Hurst, Rees, Orme, Brown, and Green, London.

- Morris D. 1985: *The Art of Ancient Cyprus, Oxford Phaidon.*

- Murray M.A. 2000: Viticulture and wine production, in: *Ancient Egyptian Materials and Technology.* (eds. P. Nicholson and I. Shaw). Cambridge University Press, 577-608.

- Nemejcová-Pavúková V. 1979: Nálezy bolerázskej skupiny z Vrbového. In: *Archeol. rozhl.*, 31, s. 393.

- Oates J. 1987: *Le Choga Mami transitional et l'Obeid 1: synthèse de la séance. In Huot, J.L. ed. La Préhistoire de la Mésopotamie*. Paris: Editions du CNRS, *1987*:199-206.

- Özgüç T. 1999: Vases used for ritual purposes from Eskiyapar. In: T. Mikasa (Hrsg.), Essays on Ancient Anatolia. *Bulletin of the Middle Eastern Culture Centre in Japan* (Wiesbaden) 1-23.

- Pernety A.J. 1758: *Dictionnaire mytho-hermétique, dans lequel on trouve les allégories fabuleuses des poètes, les métaphores, les énigmes et les termes barbares des philosophes hermétiques expliqués.* Paris.

- Ping-Yü H. & Needham J. 1959: The Laboratory Equipment of the Early Mediæval Chinese Alchemists, in: *Ambix*, 7:2, 58-112, DOI: 10. 1179.

- Platon N. 1971: *Zakros. The Discovery of a Lost Palace of Ancient Crete*, New York, Scribner.

- Platon, N. 1974: *Zakros, The New Minoan Palace (in Greek)*. The Athens Archaeological Society, Athens.

- Plinius Secundus. *Naturalis Historia*. XV, XXXIII.

- Plouvier L. 2000: Al Kindi *Kitab Kimya al-'Itr wa al Tas'idat* : *Livre sur les parfums, la chimie et la distillation*. in *L'Europe se met à table*, Bruxelles.

- Porta Gb. della 1609: *De distillationibus, libri IX*, Strasbourg.

- Puglisi D. 2010: Dal vassoio tripodato al kernos: un set di ceramiche TMIA da Haghia Triada, in *Creta Antica* 11, 45-129.

- Ray P.C. 1956: *History of chemistry in ancient and medieval India* (ed.) P. Ray (2nd ed.). Calcutta: Indian Chemical Society.

- Recke M. 2006: Eine Trickvase von der Akropolis in Perge und andere Zeugnisse für kultische Aktivitäten während der Mittel- und Spätbronzeit: Zur Rolle Pamphyliens im 2. Jahrtausend v. Chr. A. Erkanal-Öktü v.d. (ed.), *Hayat Erkanal'a Armağan. Kültürlerin Yansıması*, İstanbul 618-626.

- Françoise Rougemont 2014: Sheep Rearing Wool Production and Management in Mycenaean Written Documents in C. Breniquet, C. Michel ed. *Wool Economy in the Ancient Near East*, 340-371.

- Roquetaillade J. de, 1350: *De consideratione Quintæ essentiæ rerum omnium (*vers 1350) Traduction: *La vertu et propriété de la quintessence de toutes choses, mise en François par Antoine du Moulin Maconnais, valet de chambre de la Royne de Navarre.* Lyon, Jean de Tournes.

- Rothman M.J. 2000: *Tepe Gawra: The evolution of a small, prehistoric center in Northern Iraq,* Philadelphia.

- Rovesti P. 1980: Alla scoperta del primo alambicco del mondo: la distillazione ha cinquemila anni. *Rivista Italiana EPPOS*, LXII, 7, 342-345.

- Ryšánek J. & V. Václavû 1989: Destilační přítroj ze spišského štrvtku, *Archeologické Rozhledy*, vol. 41, 196-201.

- Ryšánek J. 1993: Extrakční přístroj z Tróje, *Archeologické Rozhledy*, vol. 45, pp. 127-133.

- Sackett *L.H. and M.* Popham 1970: Excavations at Palaikastro VII, *BSA* 65: 203–42.

- Salque M., Bogucki P.I., Pyzel J., Sobkowiak-Tabaka I., Marzena R.G. Szmyt & R.P. Evershed 2013: Earliest evidence for cheese making in the sixth millennium BC in northern Europe in *Nature* 493, 522–525.

- Samorini G. 2017: La "Donna Alambicco" e altri distillatori arcaici, in: *Erboristeria Domani*, N. 400, 76-85.

- Savonarole M. 1532: *De arte conficiendi aquam vitae*. La Haye.

- Schlíemann H. 1881: *Ilios.* Leipzig.

- Schlosser Š. 2011: Distillation from Bronze Age till today, in: J. Markoš (Ed.), *Proceedings of the 38th International Conference of Slovak Society of Chemical Engineering*, Tatranské Matliare, Slovakia, 1-12.

- Seager R. 1909: Excavations on the Island of Mochlos, Crete, in 1908, *American Journal Archaeology* 13, N° 3, 273-303.

- Shelmerdine C. Wright 1985: *The perfume Industry of Mycenaean Pylos*, Goteborg: P. Astrom Forlag.

- Slane W. K. 1986: Two deposits from the Early Roman cellar building, Corinth, *Hesperia*, vol. 55, 271 - 420.

- Smith C. and Welch F.B. 1904: *Excavations at Phylakopi in Melos-conducted by the British School at Athens*. London: Macmillan and Co.

- Smith C.S. 1965: An Examination of the Arsenic-Rich Coating on a Bronze Bull from Horoztepe, in ed. W. J. Young *Application of Science in Examination of Works of Art,* 96–102.

- Soles J.S. 1978: Mochlos. Expedition January: *Expedition Magazine*. Penn Museum, January.

- Soles J. S. & Davaras C. 1993: Excavations at Mochlos, in *Hesperia* 61-2, 413-445.

- Soles J. S. & Davaras C. 1994: Excavations at Mochlos, in *Hesperia* 63-4, 391-435.

- Soukup R.W. & Mayer H. 1997: Alchemistisches Gold, Paracelsistische Pharmaka: Laboratoriumstechnik im 16. Jahrhundert. Vol 10 *Perspektiven der Wissenschaftsgeschichte* Böhlau Verlag Wien.

- Speiser E.A. 1935: *Excavations at Tepe Gawra 1*, University of Pennsylvania - Museum of Archaeology and Anthropology.

- Sticklmair J.G. & Fair J.R. 1998: *Distillation. Principles and practice*, Wiley.

- Taylor F. Sherwood 1937: The Visions of Zosimos, *AX*, x, 88; *Symbols in Greek Alchemical Writings*, *AAX*, 64.

- Taylor F. Sherwood 1945. The evolution of the Still, in *ANS,* 5, 185.

- Taylor F. Sherwood 1950: *Alchemists, Founders of Modern Chemistry*, Henry Schuman, Inc., Publishers, New York.

- Thaddaeus Florentinus (1223-1303): De virtutibus aquae vitae alcohol: Anthropological Archaeological Perspectives, in: *Annual Review of Anthropology*, vol. 35, 229-249.

- Thurm, H.G. 1978: Shao Chui, *Gebramuer Wein im alten China.* Team-Fachvedlli. Karlstein aI M Sonderausgabe der Alkohol-Industrie, Ed.

- Tobler J.A. 1950: *Excavations at Tepe Gawra*, vol. II, The University Museum of Pennsylvania, Philadelphia.

- Valenzuela Zapata A.G., Buell P.D., de la-Paz Solano-Pérez M., and H. Park 2015: *"Huichol" Stills: A Century of Anthropology – Technology Transfer and Innovation"*.

- Von Osten S. 1992: *Das Alchemistenlaboratorium Oberstockstall. Ein Fundcomplex des 16. Jahrhunderts aus Niederosterreich*, PhD dissertation Universitata Wien.

- Wilkinson T.J. and D.J. Tucker 1995: *Settlement Development in the North Jazira, Iraq.* British School of Archaeology in Iraq. Warminster: Aris & Phillips;

- Wilson C. Anne 2006: *A history of Wine distilling and spirits 500 BC – AD 2000*, Trowbridge, Wiltshire.

http://www.eacrh.net/ojs/index.php/crossroads/article/view/42/Vol8_Huichol_html.

- Wood R.W. 1934: The Purple Gold of Tutankhamun, in *JEA* 20: 62-66.

- Zizumbo Villareal D., González Zozaya F., Olay Barrientos A., Almendros López L., Flores Pérez P. and P. Colunga García Marín 2009: Distillation in Western Mesoamerica before European Contact, *Economic Botany*, vol. 63(4), 413-426.

- Zohary D., Hopf M. 2000: *Domestication of Plants in the Old World: The Origin and Spread of Cultivated Plants in West Asia, Europe, and the Nile Valley.* Oxford: Oxford Univ Press.

www.ingramcontent.com/pod-product-compliance
Lightning Source LLC
Chambersburg PA
CBHW041516220426
43668CB00003B/36